Nonlinear Dynamics of Financial Crises

Nonlinear Dynamics of Financial Crises

How to Predict Discontinuous Decisions

Ionut Purica

AMSTERDAM • BOSTON • HEIDELBERG • LONDON
NEW YORK • OXFORD • PARIS • SAN DIEGO
SAN FRANCISCO • SINGAPORE • SYDNEY • TOKYO

Academic Press is an imprint of Elsevier

Academic Press is an imprint of Elsevier
125, London Wall, EC2Y 5AS, UK
525 B Street, Suite 1800, San Diego, CA 92101-4495, USA
225 Wyman Street, Waltham, MA 02451, USA
The Boulevard, Langford Lane, Kidlington, Oxford OX5 1GB, UK

Notices
Knowledge and best practice in this field are constantly changing. As new research and experience broaden our understanding, changes in research methods, professional practices, or medical treatment may become necessary.

Practitioners and researchers must always rely on their own experience and knowledge in evaluating and using any information, methods, compounds, or experiments described herein. In using such information or methods they should be mindful of their own safety and the safety of others, including parties for whom they have a professional responsibility.

To the fullest extent of the law, neither the Publisher nor the authors, contributors, or editors, assume any liability for any injury and/or damage to persons or property as a matter of products liability, negligence or otherwise, or from any use or operation of any methods, products, instructions, or ideas contained in the material herein.

ISBN: 978-0-12-803275-6

British Library Cataloguing-in-Publication Data
A catalogue record for this book is available from the British Library

Library of Congress Cataloging-in-Publication Data
A catalog record for this book is available from the Library of Congress

For information on all Academic Press publications,
visit our website at http://store.elsevier.com/

Working together
to grow libraries in
developing countries

www.elsevier.com • www.bookaid.org

DEDICATION

In memory of my Father

CONTENTS

In the evolution of the various financial crises, as described by Reinhart and Rogoff, the pattern of behavior that occurs is showing, first, a slow penetration of a latter predominant financial instrument that acquires credibility—and with it the absorption of more credit—by comparison to the other instruments and then the penetration saturates into a moment when risk accumulation is overcoming a given level beyond which the credibility diminishes suddenly and the decision to continue financing the said instrument takes a discontinuous turn of abandoning the allocation of credit.

From a synergetic approach, as developed by Haken in the 1980s, the description of the behavior presented above seems to be common to other situations of saturated penetration into a given niche. As an example, Fischer and Pray and later Marchetti and Nakicenovic from IIASA showed how various technologies are penetrating the niche of technologies following a logistic function—describing the process of saturation—and how the periodic occurrence of saturation of the predominant technology is generating technological cycles with various time constants.

The fashion-like behavior of the financial instruments penetration leads to the use of the notion of "memes," introduced by Dawkins and Hofstaedter as diffusion—reaction mind entities that generate the onset of various kinds of collective behavior. In the financing environment, the "financial niche," all sorts of credit instruments are generated that penetrate slowly, at first, then occupy the niche to later saturate and be replaced by others.

Till now we have identified the process of logistic penetration of memes, associated to financial instruments, into the financial niche. This describes credit associated to credibility. Further on we are showing how in this "credit space" the decision to allocate money (to finance) various types of financial instruments is taken, with a view to describe not only linear decisions but also nonlinear ones, of the type abandon financing a given instrument, that are generating financial crises.

Going further on to describing the behavior of a decision maker to allocate money to various financial instruments, we will use the ideas of Gheorghe and Purica, Ursu, Purica et al., and Purica to describe the allocation process of decision by means of a Fokker–Planck (F–P) equation stemming from a master equation of the process. The stationary solution of the F–P equation shows the existence of a potential that presents bifurcation with the variation of its coefficients associated to the benefits and the costs of risk control of the process. On this folded surface (associated to a "cusp" catastrophe in Thom's terminology) the trajectory of the financing may evolve either locally or globally showing discontinuous paths from one fold to the other, thus representing the decision to abandon financing a given instrument. This folded surface may be associated to a "credit space" where sudden "loss of credit" situations may be accommodated, along with the usual linear evolutions of the past descriptions. The determination of a "separatrix" limit and the evolution of the credit trajectory close to that limit may predict a crisis—the decision makers, be they financial regulatory bodies or governments, being in the position to prepare for absorbing the coming crisis or to take measures to avoid it. Thus, the sudden change induced by small variations of the parameters may be predicted in this approach.

The capability to describe a richer type of behavior leads to the possibility to propose a dynamic regulatory approach that results from the possibility to predict the coming of a crisis-generating decision. Comments are made on the way some crisis indicators may be introduced and the types of dynamic regulatory activity that may be associated to the process. Moreover, the identification of logistic penetration and limits of discontinuity are likely to better separate a completely free market from the moment of the triggering of a regulatory preventive limit close to the limits of discontinuity. The resilience of the system is thus increased and shocks are either absorbed or avoided with calculable costs.

This book ends with final comments on the possibility to use dynamic models in order to have a more accurate description for the evolution in the financial niche and the potential limits of freedom and controlled behavior that trigger the passage from competition to cooperation in order to increase the stability of the system.

ACKNOWLEDGMENTS

I would like to thank Prof. Ali Bayar for having created and managed ECOMOD into a platform of knowledge exchange (among other positive functions). Moreover, all my thanks go to Dr. Lester Seigel, whose long discussions about the financial world and nonlinear systems have created the insight and the understanding that allowed me to apply nonlinear models to describe the financial crisis cycle. Encouragement in this sense also came from Prof. Willi Semmler and Dr. Aquiles Almansi. Also, I want to mention Prof. Herman Haken, whose Synergetics books were opening, at least for me, the world of nonlinear behavior, and Prof. Giuseppe Furlan, who appreciated the application of Fokker-Planck equation theory to the socioeconomic and financial processes and gave me the opportunity to do research on the process. I must also acknowledge Prof. Adrian Gheorghe, Acad. Mircea Malita, and Acad. Solomon Marcus for their support in my early endeavor to develop nonlinear models, as well as Acad. Aurel Iancu for his guidance. I am leaving my family at the end to have the chance to express all my gratitude for my wife and kids, who have supported my writing of this book.

CHAPTER *1*

Introduction

This chapter reviews some ideas on limits, crises, complex behavior, and local versus global perception that serve to create the necessary state of mind (memes in Dawkins terminology) to make the reader curious about the rest of the book.

In November 1997 the financial crisis of that time had already started in Mexico and the Asian Tigers were having problems. Moreover, Russia was entering the crisis situation too. The bifurcation related to the change from one state to the other—in the case of stock exchange, from "sell" to "buy" is an indication of a change in the traders' collective behavior that is triggered by small changes of perceived parameters' evolution. The euphoria of a seemingly endless exponential growth of some financial instruments is replaced suddenly by the sorrow of a saturation followed by abandoning the allocation of money to some instruments and the shift toward others.

There is an important message here that is the fact that people have in their minds some given states and external information is almost unconsciously interpreted as either going toward one or the other, without anything in between. This behavior is produced by some entities of the mind having similar properties with genes whose conceptualization had been done by Dawkins who also coined the name "meme" for them.

Actually, in a booklet titled "Modern Money Mechanics," the Federal Reserve Bank of Chicago says: "What, then, makes these instruments—checks, paper money, and coins—acceptable at face value in payment of all debts and for other monetary uses? Mainly, it is the confidence people have that they will be able to exchange such money for other financial assets and real goods and services whenever they choose to do so. This partly is a matter of law; currency has been designated "legal tender" by the government—that is, it must be accepted."

As we see the basis of money use is about credibility, a concept that relates to people's minds and this is based on memes dynamics.

We will explain more of this in what follows related to the penetration of financial instruments (portfolio components) used in the cultural niches of the financial system.

Application of the notion of meme in the financial environment in relation to the financial instruments leads to the idea of a cultural niche (in the sense of Popper) of financial instruments associated to memes. At each moment in time there are several instruments in the niche but, dynamically, one of them has the tendency to occupy the niche in a logistic way—that is, until it saturates and decays while another instrument takes its place as dominant.

Logistic penetration was used for biological species in competition by Verhulst (1838) and for the penetration of technologies (Marchetti and Nakicenovic's 1978 work at International Institute for Applied Systems Analysis, IIASA, is relevant), as well as Sornette and Cauwels (2012) and others in looking at the development of Internet companies, for example.

By contrast to Malthus (1798), who advocated the exponential growth of the population in a world where resources were not available with the same speed, Verhulst (1838) had introduced the notion of saturation, given by the limit of the environment where species are in competition. The fact that we live in a world having limits has then been discussed by various economists, among which we mention Kenneth Ewart Boulding (1966) who said:

> I am tempted to call the open economy the "cowboy economy," the cowboy being symbolic of the illimitable plains and also associated with reckless, exploitative, romantic, and violent behavior, which is characteristic of open societies. The closed economy of the future might similarly be called the "spaceman" economy, in which the earth has become a single spaceship, without unlimited reservoirs of anything, either for extraction or for pollution, and in which, therefore, man must find his place in a cyclical ecological system which is capable of continuous reproduction of material form even though it cannot escape having inputs of energy.

Later on he concludes:

> Anyone who believes exponential growth can go on forever in a finite world is either a madman or an economist.

Going along with Ramos-Martín and Ortega-Cerdà we may say that over half a century ago, Schumpeter (1949) understood nonlinear evolutionary development and discontinuity by means of his theory of creative destruction. This idea has been later named "punctuated equilibrium" by some analysts (Gowdy, 1994), using the same term that is in use in paleontology to describe this stepwise evolution (Eldredge and Gould, 1972; Gould and Eldredge, 1993).

One way of analyzing the existence of this discontinuity is by means of a phase diagram. This methodology has been used in the case of CO_2 emissions (Unruh and Moomaw, 1998), and in the case of energy intensity (De Bruyn, 1999; Ramos-Martín 1999, 2001). The phase diagrams are intended to show whether the evolution of certain variables, over time, is stable (even dynamically stable) or divergent. Thus, one may find if there are attractor points or not. If so, we can check how persistent are those attractors as well as the magnitude of the fluctuations around them (Unruh and Moomaw, 1998). In what follows we will show that there is a phase change behavior resulting from the penetration of memes associated to financial instruments.

A potential approach is a time-evolving space in which we monitor the evolution of the variable. This representation allows us to see whether we are facing a "punctuated equilibrium"-like behavior or not. If we are, then we will see how the variable concentrates around certain attractors. If not, the evolution of the variable will be different, showing a more complex, possibly discontinuous, behavior. This means that in the process of development, we should focus empirical research on identifying the attractor points and the system evolution trajectory from one to the other.

This situation leads to a series of "bifurcation" points (Prigogine, 1987), in which, for given boundary conditions, there are several stable solutions. Following Faber and Proops (1998) a "bifurcation may occur when the stable equilibrium for a dynamic system is sensitive to changes in the parameters of the system." Thus, when the parameter goes beyond a critical threshold, the system becomes sensitive to sudden change and therefore unstable. In this case, tiny perturbations may trigger drastic changes (Dalmazzone, 1999), leading to a set of new different stable equilibriums to which the system might eventually flip. We have just mentioned some authors; actually the literature has developed various examples of nonlinear behavior.

There is a further step to the process, that is, the decision to finance each instrument that is taken by the decision makers in the banks (or other financial entities), which are generally called the markets. This is dependent on the perception by the decision maker of the financial instruments' dynamic, seen as memes in a niche. The transition probabilities of the master equation of the process are determined by the logistic behavior, bringing a similarity to the Ising process in physics. The decision process is described by the stationary solution of the associated Fokker–Planck equation that shows bifurcation.

This further allows us to represent the behavior of the decision to allocate money to financial instruments in a three-dimensional space described as a cusp catastrophe in Rene Thom's terminology. The decision is seen as a trajectory that may have a smooth evolution, or a discontinuous one, when passing from a fold to another. The discontinuous case means that a given instrument will not be financed any longer or, in other words, that a meme will have reached saturation in the niche and the decision maker will abandon allocating money to that financial instrument.

If we look back, one may see "dot com's" were like this, "housing" was like this, as well as other various crises in history as nicely described by Reinhart and Rogoff (2009).

A profound insight into the crisis dynamics was done by Galbraith (1994). His phrase "Financial genius is before the fall" is a synthesis of the process.

He identified both the upward-going phase (that we call exponential growth) and the sudden end (which we describe as a discontinuous decision resulting from saturation in the logistic penetration of the dominant financial instrument). On the upward trend he said:

Although only a few observers have noted the vested interest in error that accompanies speculative euphoria, it is, nonetheless, an extremely plausible phenomenon. Those involved with the speculation are experiencing an increase in wealth — getting rich or being further enriched. No one wishes to believe that this is fortuitous or undeserved; all wish to think it is the result of their own superior insight or intuition. The very increase in values thus captures the thoughts and minds of those being rewarded. Speculation buys up, in a very practical way, the intelligence of those involved.

He also coined the dynamics of the sudden end of the euphoria:

Something, it matters little what — although it will always be much debated — triggers the ultimate reversal. Those who had been riding the upward wave decide now is the time to get out. Those who thought the increase would be forever find their illusion destroyed abruptly, and they, also, respond to the newly revealed reality by selling or trying to sell. Thus the collapse, And thus the rule, supported by the experience of centuries: the speculative episode always ends not with a whimper but with a bang.

We see another description of a logistic penetration of memes that starts with contaminating the minds of people (in the financial world and not only) then reaches saturation and the inherent discontinuous decision to abandon the previous behavior and divert resources to something else.

The approach we have taken allows us to see the evolution of the decision to allocate money not just as a linear one but to be able to view—and thus predict—a larger type of cases, including the discontinuous one, that are perceived as crises. Moreover, one may understand the various ways to get out of the crisis—that is, if one cannot avoid the first shock, the return can be either smooth, more adaptive, that takes more time, but does not induce another large shock, or in a direct manner that needs a very resilient economy to absorb the resulting shocks.

Also, the capacity to predict allows a new way of monitoring the evolution of decisions such as not to cross the border of discontinuity, inducing a crisis, or to be prepared in advance when crossing it. A complementary type of monitoring procedures may thus be introduced with the aim of predicting the near-crisis situations with enough advance time to take appropriate measures.

There is one more notion to stress here. It is the difference between the local and the global view of the system's behavior. Looking in a small neighborhood around the evolution trajectory one may see only a local trend that may prove to be discontinuously different if enlarging the neighborhood to the entire system.

A proverb says that one should not lose sight of the woods because of the trees. It seems that financial crises have a tendency to lose sight of the full picture because of the short-term effects of some instruments.

One of the best artistic illustrations of such different behavior is represented in a lithograph called "Waterfall," by M.C. Escher (Bool et al., 1982). Concentrating on the watercourse in this lithograph leaves the sensation that the flow is done downward at all times. While looking at the full picture, it shows the flow is going up and a waterfall is created.

In the same way, the decision trajectories to allocate money to financial instruments may seem to converge to a stable attractor if looking at the local behavior; while if one looks at the full decisions' space the trajectories may reach a discontinuous path that means a decision to abandon a given financial instrument.

Let us see now how all the above unfolds into a full-fledged explanation of the process.

We will show how memes can have a change of phase type of behavior in their reaction with one another. From this, the dynamic described by the logistic equation comes as a natural outcome. The data from the last crisis fit the logistic penetration of financial instruments and the decision to allocate resources to a new instrument is described with a master equation that leads to a Fokker–Planck equation whose stationary solution is pointing to an evolution of decision trajectories on a cusp-like surface having a limit of discontinuity that may sometimes be crossed. This is perceived as a crisis. Monitoring the derivative of the logistic function may provide a way to predict the moment the exponential growth changes to saturation and thus, to be prepared for the discontinuous decision to reallocate resources or, alternatively, to take measures to avoid crossing the limit of discontinuity.

REFERENCES

Bool, F.H., Kist, J.R., Locher, J.L., Wierda, F., with essays by Ernst, B., Escher, M.C., 1982. In: Locher, J.L. (Ed.), M.C. Escher: His Life and Complete Graphic Work With a Fully Illustrated Catalogue. Harry N. Abrams, Inc. Publishers, New York, NY. ISBN: 0810908581 (M.C. Escher, Waterfall, 1961, Lithograph 380 × 300 (15″ × 113/4″), Compare cat. no. 438).

Boulding, K.W., 1966. The economics of the coming spaceship earth. In: Jarrett, H. (Ed.), Environmental Quality in a Growing Economy. Resources for the Future/Johns Hopkins University Press, Baltimore, MD, pp. 3–14.

Dalmazzone, S., 1999. Economic Activity and the Resilience of Ecological Systems (Ph.D. thesis). University of York.

de Bruyn, S.M., 1999. The need to change attractors. Ökologisches Wirtschaften 3, 15–17.

Eldredge, N., Gould, J.S., 1972. Punctuated equilibria: an alternative to phyletic gradualism. In: Schopf, T.J.M. (Ed.), Models in Paleobiology. Freeman, Cooper and Co., San Francisco, CA.

Faber, M., Proops, J.L.R., 1998. Evolution, Time, Production and the Environment. Springer, Berlin.

Galbraith, J.K., 1994. A Short History of Financial Euphoria. Penguin Books, pp. 4–5. ISBN: 0140238565.

Gould, S.J., Eldredge, N., 1993. Punctuated equilibrium comes of age. Nature 366, 223–227.

Gowdy, J.M., 1994. Coevolutionary Economics: The Economy, Society, and the Environment. Kluwer Academic Publishers, Amsterdam.

Malthus, T.R., 1798. An Essay on the Principle of Population as It Affects the Future Improvement of Society. Published for J. Johnson, London.

Marchetti, C., Nakicenovic, N., 1978. The Dynamics of Energy Systems and the Logistic Substitution Model. IIASA AR 78, 18.

Modern Money Mechanics, A Workbook on Bank Reserves and Deposit Expansion, Federal Reserve Bank of Chicago (This complete booklet was originally produced and distributed free by Public Information Center Federal Reserve Bank of Chicago, P.O. Box 834 Chicago, IL 60690-0834, telephone: 312 322 5111).

Prigogine, I., 1987. Exploring complexity. Eur. J. Oper. Res. 30, 97–103.

Ramos-Martín, J., 1999. Breve comentario sobre la desmaterialización en el estado español. Ecología Política 18, 61–64.

Ramos-Martín, J., 2001. Historical analysis of energy intensity of Spain: from a "conventional view" to an "integrated assessment." Popul. Environ. 22, 281–313.

Ramos-Martín, J., Ortega-Cerdà, M. Non-Linear Relationship Between Energy Intensity and Economic Growth, Paper submitted to the ESEE Conference Frontiers 2, held in Tenerife, Spain, 12–15 February 2003.

Reinhart, C.M., Rogoff, K.S., 2009. This Time Is Different: Eight Centuries of Financial Folly. Princeton University Press, Princeton, NJ, ISBN: 9780691142166.

Schumpeter, J.A., 1949. The Theory of Economic Development. Harvard University Press, Cambridge, MA.

Sornette, D., Cauwels, P., 2012. The Illusion of the Perpetual Money Machine, Notenstein Academy White Paper Series. <http://arxiv.org/abs/1212.2833> and <http://ssrn.com/abstract=2191509>.

Unruh, G.C., Moomaw, W.R., 1998. An alternative analysis of apparent EKC-type transitions. Ecol. Econ. 25, 221–229.

Verhulst, P.-F., 1838. Notice sur la loi que la population poursuit dans son accroissement. Correspondance mathématique et physique 10, 113–121.

CHAPTER 2

Evolution of Financial Crises

This chapter reviews the description of the crisis-like behavior and identifies common patterns of crises. Further, there is a review of approaches from general equilibrium to complex systems to evolutionary economics interpretation of crises that are destined to provide the present state of the art on crises modeling attempts to date.

When a general of the Roman Empire was coming home victorious, he was acclaimed by the crowds, in a triumph parade, where he would ride in his chariot in front of his soldiers. There was, though, in the chariot behind the general, a man who kept telling the general, "do not forget that you are a mortal."

In our dynamic world of today, it seems we have somehow lost this feedback and in our strive for "a triumph," be it in an obscure office or on Wall Street, we refuse to be aware that eventually things come to saturation and then to sudden change.

Several things are stemming out of the above example. First there is a wish for success given by promoting a given idea of, for example, a financial instrument. Most of the time the idea is not one's own but a reaction with the business environment where such an idea has diffused from one mind to the other generating a "phase change" that triggers the second element associated with a collective behavior. The process was initially identified by Dawkins, and the elements of evolution of the mind based on imitation, replication, and diffusion were called memes.

This is the "exponential growth" trend. The euphoric belief associated to this trend is that "the sky is the limit," obviously meaning that there is no limit. But, even the sky *is* a limit, seemingly a remote one, but still a limit.

In going toward the limit, whatever that is, a moment comes when the trend changes to saturation ("remember you are a mortal"). Once saturation sets in, the meme associated with the trend becomes "untenable," "old fashioned," and whatever other term you may want to find in relation to its credibility. The decision about supporting that meme (including financial support) is suddenly shifting to abandoning it.

Finally a new meme (materialized in a financial instrument) comes in and takes the dominant position among the other existing instruments (memes). The simultaneous existence of competing memes (financial instruments) takes place in a niche (in the sense of Popper), more exactly, in the case of financial instruments, in a "financial cultural niche."

How does the above apply to a financial crisis from the phase change in the penetration of the new instrument to the decision to abandon it?

2.1 DEFINITIONS AND COMMON PATTERNS OF THE CRISIS

The term "financial crisis" is defined as "a wider range of disturbances, such as sharp declines in asset prices, failures of large financial intermediaries, or disruption in foreign exchange markets" (De Bonis et al., 1999).

Allen and Snyder (2009) are synthetizing the characteristics of the crisis. They consider that "crisis" is perceived as a serious impact on the real economy, including employment, production, and purchasing power, along with the possibility that great numbers of households and firms or even governments are unable to meet their obligations (insolvency).

An example of a "vicious cycle" may start from a money-liquidity crisis at some banks, which extends to an international crisis of investor confidence in the financial sector, leading to a balance of payments problem for the country and currency devaluation, that, therefore, generates even further liquidity problems and, further on, solvency crises for the banks.

Several authors, including Soros (2008), Allen and Snyder (2009), Semmler and Bernard (2012), are doing extensive analysis of models to describe the crisis cycle. One of the conclusions related to the 2007 crisis was that there is a lack of appropriate models that would be able to predict discontinuous behavior.

Models of financial crises are characterized as "first-generation" or "second-generation" or, in the last years, "third-generation."

The models of first-generation class, as developed by Krugman (1979) and others, underline the importance of a country's foreign exchange reserves. That is, if government budget deficits are too big, then ultimately a government loses the ability to maintain these reserves, and a speculative attack on its currency exchange rate is inevitable.

Second-generation models, described by Rangvid (2001), were developed during the 1990s when the above cause–effect assumption could not explain various currency crises. There is now a different relationship between economic parameters such as public sector deficits and the timing and importance of speculative currency attacks and associated instabilities. The moment of government decisions to abandon a currency regime in favor of other political-economic objectives had also proved difficult to predict. Second-generation models look for "multiple equilibriums" that key variables might pass through, unpredictable or irrational behavior of private investors and governments, and there has been an effort to discover new "sunspot variables" that will better explain sudden changes in markets.

The idea of multiple equilibriums is bringing this class of models closer to nonlinearity, but the idea of hidden variables is a reminiscence of understanding a model as a formula, whose parameters are usually determined by a regression done on some data series. We must mention here that a model, in our opinion, should be a description of the process that may lead to a differential equation (or a system of) whose solution (be it stationary or dynamic) is associated to a space having several basins of behavior (attractors) where the system evolution trajectory (Poincare) may pass at different times. Starting by assuming a formula, even if by chance a correct one for a given basin of behavior, and pouring in as many variables as possible to check potential correlations may result in some capability to predict. But this is limited to that basin of behavior or a portion of it; if the system's trajectory moves to a different basin of behavior (attractor) then the first model is not valid any longer. The trend, if not to change the formula, is to put more variables in. This may lead to extending the description and having prediction capability on a new portion of the basin of behavior, but the integrated picture is still not seen.

Third-generation models, as per Krugman (1999) and Allen et al. (2002), introduce additional variables and feedback processes, especially the role of companies', entrepreneurs', and governments' balance sheets, and the impact of international financial flows and exchange rates on those balance sheets. During and after the 1997 Asian financial crises, the financial condition of firms went down more than anticipated by second-generation models, which drew attention to these processes. Moreover, it has been difficult for economies to return to normal growth and stability.

A more extended description of models is given in Appendix 1 with some comments on their position related to a nonlinear approach to the problem.

2.2 THE CRISIS CYCLE BIRD'S-EYE DESCRIPTION

One of the things most authors agree upon is the existence of a "boom–bust" cycle; we call it crisis cycle. The pattern of behavior is associated with a phase of growth—boom—in financial activity (of course connected to economic evolution) followed by a sharp fall—bust—in the variables' values, which is normally attributed to loss of credibility in the former dominant pattern of behavior.

In most cases of large-scale financial crisis, a country or region starts with the advantage given by increasing supplies of base money, "quasi-money" that are created from base money, and credit supplies associated with financial liberalization and deregulation.

That country or region may, for a given time, benefit from foreign direct investment (FDI), making the banking system, including government, well capitalized and able to increase money liquidity. Assets values increase and interest rates are low. This leads to more consumption, investment, borrowing, and government spending that support economic growth. There is a "boom," as measured by increased monetary wealth held by private and public sectors of an economy, including the value of real estate, currency reserves, stocks, etc., and/or the gross domestic product (GDP).

Then, the supply of base money (M) times its velocity of circulation for GDP purposes (v) shrinks, and consequently, so does the equivalent nominal GDP. The decline in nominal GDP is usually split between its two components: (i) real GDP, which is the volume of current production (Q); and (ii) the GDP price level (p).

These variables are linked by the equation of exchange:

$$Mv = Qp$$

When Q decreases for a continuous period (e.g., at least 6 months) it is called a recession, and when p declines there is deflation. After this process begins, monetary policymakers may react by rapidly expanding (M). It is though possible that this action may come too late—international confidence in the country or region may be damaged already: individuals and institutional entities may have nonpayable debts, banks may be failing, etc. In this case, which is typical in countries with weak financial systems, the increase in M may reverse the trend of p and possibly produce hyperinflation, but Q would continue to fall. Moreover, a weak financial system may be unable to sustain the circulation rate of secure currencies for productive activities, and thus v would decrease.

The initial contraction in basic money (Mv) in a crisis may be due to monetary authorities or national and international investors taking away money (M) from the country, or there may be a decline in v because of the inability of the financial system to allocate money to productive activities.

One synergetic approach to the velocity of rotation of the monetary mass is found in Purica (2010), where an equation similar to the Schrodinger in quantum mechanics is found and it is shown that once one state of equilibrium is exited the system goes to another state of equilibrium differing from the first by a "quantized" quantity—that is, the system cannot occupy any operational level but discrete ones. The passage from one level to another can be perceived as a potential crisis.

A contraction in basic money or withdrawal of international investment may undermine debt markets, bank capital, equity markets, or government reserves; consequently, monetary wealth is revalued downward. General economic or political uncertainty worsens the situation—the resulting austerity-mentality causes a contraction of spending and credit, and an increased "risk premium" attached to business activity scares away investment and bank lending.

If interest rates rise, the demand for quasi-money and credit declines and people try to convert the monetary "toxicity" into more secure base money. No reserve-currency banking system is able to cover all of its monetary toxic assets with secure bank reserves if customers try to redeem too much of the money at once, and this can destroy the banks themselves.

A deteriorating banking sector may be unable to honor its deposits, bad loan problems show up, and a "lender of last resort" such as the central bank, taxpayers (Main Street as it was called in 2007), or the International Monetary Fund (IMF) may need to be found.

Reinhart and Rogoff (2007, 2009) have shown that the current crisis fits many historical patterns, as explained next with emphasis on the US situation. For example, Reinhart and Rogoff (2007) show that:

> ... the run-up in US housing and equity prices that Kaminsky and Reinhart (1999) find to be the best leading indicators of crisis in countries experiencing large capital inflows closely tracks the average of the previous 18 post-World War II banking crises in industrial countries (p. 339).

2.3 EVOLUTIONARY ECONOMICS AND COMPLEX SYSTEMS APPROACHES TO DESCRIBING CRISIS CYCLES

2.3.1 General Equilibrium Economic Theory and Financial Crises

The neoclassical general equilibrium model has long provided the theoretical rationale underlying mainstream economic efforts to understand macroeconomic fluctuations. This model conceives of an economy as a set of fully connected interlocking markets, which can be analyzed like a force field in physics. We should mention that one other such attempt was done by Spiru Haret in his *Social Mechanics* book published in 1910. To make the model work one must assume that the market participants are homogeneous or nearly so. The model presumes it would be in equilibrium unless some exogenous force was to disturb it, in which case it would normally return quickly to equilibrium.

But nominal and institutional rigidities are assumed to prevent such shocks from being perfectly damped, which generates business fluctuations. Markets in a model like this satisfy the efficient markets hypothesis and (because of the strong equilibrium tendencies) have price changes that are Gaussian (normally) distributed. So a possible extension would be to assume the model may accommodate small amplitude fluctuation that is of a "white noise" type.

An important feature of a Gaussian distribution is that very large positive and very large negative deviations from the mean (more than three standard deviations) are having very low probabilities. Yet price changes of these magnitudes routinely occur during financial crises. This suggests that whatever is occurring during these episodes is not following the processes embodied in the general equilibrium model.

The general equilibrium model also assumes that promises are always fulfilled: when goods are purchased or loans are made, the goods get paid for and the loans get repaid on schedule. This condition is routinely violated in a financial crisis. Leijonhufvud (2004) notes that, despite the obvious importance of understanding better such breakdowns in the equilibrating processes, which can threaten the social order, modern macroeconomics sheds little light on their nature. LeRoy (2004), in his survey of traditional economic analyses of price bubbles, comes to a similar conclusion.

2.3.2 Complexity Theory and Financial Crises

Given the inability of standard general equilibrium theory to explain the occurrence of financial crises, other approaches have been explored. One promising approach is to look at the economic system through the lens of complexity theory.

A complex system differs in important ways from the general equilibrium system of neoclassical economics. If an economy is a complex system, behavior is resulting as collectively generated from the actions of individual agents. Because agent behaviors interact in nonlinear ways, the collective behavior result that emerges can have a life of its own that is not obviously deducible from the properties of the agents: the whole is not only greater than the sum of the parts, but it is also different.

The effects of small changes may sometimes be amplified into large events with significant influence (the metaphor is "the butterfly effect"). Complex systems are path-dependent, that is, their present state is determined by what happened to them in the past (memory). They exhibit dynamic change: new behaviors and structures constantly stimulate more of the same. Their dynamic stability may occur far from equilibrium and may have limited lifetimes.

Dynamics dominates statics; the system evolves and adapts rather than just "running" as general equilibrium models tend to do. As a consequence, a complex system is rarely in equilibrium. It may have long periods of stability, but stability is not the same as equilibrium: it can degenerate into chaotic behavior at short notice without exogenous disturbance. This often signals what is known as a phase shift, whereby the system changes from one way of functioning to a distinctly different way.

Financial crises can often be thought of as phase shifts as we will see below. Because a complex system does not have strong tendencies to equilibrium, it does not usually generate variables with Gaussian distributions. Instead, it tends to produce power law distributions, which have fatter tails than the Gaussian and thus explain the frequent occurrence of extreme positive and negative values.

Benoit Mandelbrot (Mandelbrot and Hudson, 2004) has studied financial system prices for a long time and has produced persuasive evidence that they follow power law distributions. His work, long ignored by efficient market analysts, is now widely recognized and has been brought to the attention of the general public by Nassim Taleb (2007).

2.3.3 Complex Adaptive Systems

The mathematics of complex systems has been studied for some time now and is reasonably well understood. Although phase shifts and cascades are suggestive of financial crises and power laws are consistent with frequent large price changes, complex systems were originally developed to explain inanimate phenomena such as chemical reactions. The agents in that type of complex system have no volition of their own: they passively respond to whatever natural forces affect them.

An economy, on the other hand, is composed of agents who both perceive their situation and are capable of changing their behavior in response to it. This suggests the notion of a complex adaptive system where the agents are active participants. The behavior of such a system, although more difficult to represent, would be more appropriate for the modern economy behavior. This is an endeavor that must be undertaken if we are to make progress understanding financial crises. The approach taken in this book is actually taking advantage of the developments in psychology, chemistry, and physics to arrive at a coherent description of crisis cycles based on such processes as memes reaction diffusion, phase change, logistic penetration, Fokker–Planck equation, and catastrophe theory.

The synergetic principles developed by Haken (1975, 1981, 1983) are not only introducing the master slave dynamical systems but also state an important idea: if a given behavior encountered in one system is better described in another, then the description can be applied, with a proper redefinition of the variables and parameters in the first system. So, in the text that follows we will use all the below ideas to make a coherent description of the crisis cycle that was seen to show a specific pattern of behavior.

   i. memes replicators—introduced by Dawkins in 1976,
  ii. nonlinear chemical systems with phase change—such as those analyzed by Prigogine and Nicolis,
 iii. logistic penetration—that was started by Verhulst in the middle of the nineteenth century, in contrast with the Malthus' exponential growth, and extensively applied by Marchetti and others at International Institute for Applied Systems Analysis (IIASA),
 iv. decision processes with associated master equations and Fokker–Planck equations,
  v. catastrophe theory conceptualized by Thom at the beginning of the 1970s.

Before passing on, we must remark the work of Foster (2005), who has developed a useful taxonomy for complexity systems. He identifies four types:

1. First-order (imposed energy)—Found in inanimate settings when energy is imposed on chemical elements, characterized by fractal patterns, butterfly effects, etc. Can be modeled with dynamical mathematics. This is the approach Mandelbrot applied to financial prices. The agents react passively, so this is a complex system.
2. Second-order (imposed knowledge, acquired energy)—Found in organic settings. Plants and animals receive imposed (genetically encoded) knowledge and also gain knowledge from experience. All of this gets translated into a knowledge structure that permits some control over energy acquisition. Agents both react and adapt to their environment, so this is a complex adaptive system.
3. Third-order (acquired knowledge)—Agents interact not only with their environment but also with images of possible worlds, that is, mental models. When this happens, some mental models will wind up determining aspects of reality. This is a complex adaptive system where "adaptive" involves creativity. If everyone has a mental model of the market and begins associating with his or her fellow agents according to market rules, the market gets transformed from mental model into reality.
4. Fourth-order (interactive knowledge)—At this stage mental models begin interacting with each other. Agents imagine what other agents might be imagining and alter their own models accordingly in a

potentially infinite regression. Agents form aspirations and commitments into the future. This type of complex adaptive system gets extremely complicated and depends heavily on trust and understanding to achieve the cooperation necessary for the system to function. In the study of financial crises, the first-order type of complex system is of interest because it provides realistic description of how prices behave in bubbles and panics. However, it provides little in the way of a behavioral explanation for these price changes. The fourth-order type does provide a basis for the behavioral explanation we seek. The problem is that fourth-order complex systems cannot at present be analyzed mathematically. However, though analytical solutions are at present not possible, such systems can be fruitfully studied through simulation methods and through certain types of econometric modeling, as detailed below.

The statements made above regarding the mathematical analysis of fourth-order systems are just a point in the development of the approach to describing crisis cycles. We are trying below to build some cases where analytical solutions exist and are of use to understanding (i.e., being able to predict) the system.

It seems that the idea of getting models of the same behavior from other systems was put forward in a 2006 Federal Reserve conference on systemic risk (Kambhu et al., 2007) that saw experts from various fields such as disease control, national security, civil engineering, ecology, and finance discuss their approaches to catastrophe control. The following picture emerged: an initial shock (possibly a seemingly insignificant one) leads to a coordinated behavior in the system with reinforcing (positive) feedbacks. A contagion begins, which spreads the original shock. When the pressure becomes too much the system makes a phase shift "from a stable state to an inferior stable state while shedding energy so that it cannot readily recover its original state, a process known as hysteresis" (Kambhu et al., 2007, p. 7). Research is focusing on factors that increase resistance to phase shifts and hysteresis and on factors that can help the system recover. Part of this research may prove helpful in managing financial crises.

2.4 EVOLUTIONARY ECONOMICS

If an economy is a complex adaptive system then its form and structure evolve. While the mechanism is the metaphor of the general equilibrium economy, the living organism is the one for the complex adaptive system economy.

In a neoclassical model of an evolving economy based on past history, the parameter values are always becoming obsolete—slowly or even, sometimes, very fast when there is a structural change.

Schumpeter's idea that creative destruction is the essence of capitalism is at the basis of much modern thinking in evolutionary economics. Schumpeter emphasized the role of liberal credit as a driver of speculative booms, and sudden credit contraction as a major contributor to the severity of the ensuing crash (Leathers and Raines, 2004).

The version of evolutionary economics that appears most prone to analyzing financial crises is the "Micro-Meso-Macro" framework of Dopfer et al. (2004). This framework centers on two novel concepts: (1) rules; and (2) meso units. As we shall see, these concepts are close to the meme one. And they are somehow paving the way toward understanding how memes work in the cultural niche. In this approach, a meso is a structural pattern associated to a rule. In our conceptual introduction of memes-based systems the structures (to read dynamic structures) emerge from the interaction (reaction, diffusion, etc.) of memes and depending on the systems taken into consideration (finance, technology, etc.) the dynamic structures are forming and evolve inside the systems based on such supports as financial instruments, energy conversion technologies, etc.

Continuing with Dopfer, a rule is a pattern that agents follow in their everyday economic behavior: it may be behavioral, cognitive, technological, organizational, institutional, sociocultural, etc. Rules may be nested in other rules: we might talk about a car rule that includes engine rules, tire rules, etc. or a market rule that includes a double auction rule, a fixed-price rule, etc. Rules are put in practice by microeconomic agents (individuals, families, organizations, etc.). A meso unit is a rule plus its population of actualizations (e.g., the car meso is the car rule plus all agents who make, sell, repair, or drive cars). An economic system (assumed to be complex adaptive) is a collection of meso units evolving over time. Macroeconomic behavior is the result of interactions among meso units.

Economic evolution is the process by which new rules originate and diffuse through the population: very often this process takes the form of a logistic growth path in the new rule's meso unit. Structural change occurs when a new meso rule permanently alters the coordination structure of the meso units of the economic system. Over time, creative destruction occurs: new rules are constantly being originated; the successful ones develop strong mesos, which displace previously dominant mesos; the weak ones disappear.

In this framework, a bubble or crisis in the financial sector would be analyzed as a structural change. Foster and Wild (1999a, 1999b) are inferring that logistic penetration is associated with structural change and are identifying early warning signals that the macro economy may be about to undergo a structural change. A high priority today is to analyze the international growth of money and credit over recent decades using these techniques.

REFERENCES

Allen, M., Rosenberg, C., Keller, C., Setser, B., Roubini, N., 2002. A Balance Sheet Approach to Financial Crisis, Working Paper No. 02/210. International Monetary Fund, Washington, DC.

Allen, R.E., Snyder, D., 2009. New thinking on the financial crisis. Crit. Perspect. Int. Bus. 5 (1–2), 36–55.

Dawkins, R., 1976. The Selfish Gene. Oxford, Oxford University Press (new edition with additional material, 1989, 30 years anniversary edition, 2006).

De Bonis, R., Giustiniani, A., Gomel, G., 1999. Crises and bail-outs of banks and countries: linkages, analogies, and differences. World Econ. 22 (1), 55–86.

Dopfer, K., Foster, J., Potts, J., 2004. Micro, meso, macro. J. Evol. Econ. 14, 263–279.

Foster, J., 2005. From simplistic to complex systems in economics. Cambridge J. Econ. 29, 873–892.

Foster, J., Wild, P., 1999a. Detecting self-organizational change in economic processes exhibiting logistic growth. J. Evol. Econ. 9, 109–133.

Foster, J., Wild, P., 1999b. Econometric modeling in the presence of evolutionary change. Cambridge J. Econ. 23, 749–770.

Haken, H., 1975. Co-operative phenomena in systems far from thermal equilibrium and in nonphysical systems. Rev. Mod. Phys. 47 (1).

Haken, H., 1981. Synergetics, Introduction. Springer Verlag, Berlin.

Haken, H., 1983. Synergetics, Advanced Topics. Springer Verlag, Berlin.

Kambhu, J., Weidman, S., Krishnan, N., 2007. New Directions for Understanding Systemic Risk: A Report on a Conference Co-sponsored by the Federal Reserve Bank of New York and the National Academy of Sciences. National Academies Press, Washington, DC.

Kaminsky, G.L., Reinhart, C.M., 1999. The twin crises: the causes of banking and balance of payments problems. Am. Econ. Rev. 89 (3), 473–500.

Krugman, P., 1979. A model of balance-of-payment crises. Int. Tax Public Finance 6 (4), 459–472.

Krugman, P., 1999. Balance sheets, the transfer problem and financial crises. J. Money Credit Banking 11, 311–325.

Leathers, C.G., Raines, J.P., 2004. The Schumpeterian role of financial innovations in the new economy's business cycle. Cambridge J. Econ. 28 (5), 667–681.

Leijonhufvud, A., 2004. Celebrating Ned. J. Econ. Lit. XLII, 820–821.

LeRoy, S.F., 2004. Rational exuberance. J. Econ. Lit. XLII, 801–803.

Mandelbrot, B., Hudson, R., 2004. The Misbehavior of Markets. Basic Books, New York, NY.

Purica, I., 2010. Nonlinear Models for Economic Decision Processes. Imperial College Press, London, ISBN: 9781848164277.

Rangvid, J., 2001. Second generation models of currency crises. J. Econ. Surv. 15 (5), 613–646.

Reinhart, C.M., Rogoff, K.S., 2007. Is the 2007 US sub-prime financial crisis so different? An international historical pattern. Am. Econ. Rev. 98 (2), 339–344.

Reinhart, C.M., Rogoff, K.S., 2009. This Time Is Different: A Panoramic View of Eight Centuries of Financial Crises, NBER, Working Paper, No. 13761. NBER, Cambridge, MA.

Semmler, W., Bernard, L., 2012. Boom–bust cycles: Leveraging, complex securities, and asset prices. J. Econ. Behav. Organ. 81, 442–465.

Soros, G., 2008. Noua paradigm a pietelor financiare: criza creditelor din 2008 si implicatiile ei, Ed. Litera International, Bucuresti. ISBN: 9789736754944.

Taleb, N., 2007. The Black Swan. Random House, New York, NY.

CHAPTER 3

The Sociocultural Niche

This chapter introduces the notion of meme and of cultural niche applied to financial systems and creative buildup of financial instruments. The various reaction processes of memes are described with a chemical model that shows phase transition-like behavior of new memes penetration. Further on, the resulting dynamic equation is having a logistic type of solution, and the penetration of financial instruments from 2001 to 2007 is shown to observe the logistic behavior.

3.1 CREATIVITY

When we wish to describe by a mathematical model a concept specific to the human activity, such as the concept of "creativity," for example, in the financial domain, we may relate it to the individual psychology, but at the same time we have to consider its social effects.

In the model that follows the creativity specifies the transition from activities that accommodate empirical facts to new financial instruments. From the point of view of the individual psychology this moment of transition is characterized by the sensation of surprise of discovery materialized in the language by the expression of the type "Aha!"

To appreciate the social effects of the creative activities we must begin our description by the idea that an individual is a member of a social group. The social group is also characterized by the "intellectual cohesion" of its individual members. The intellectual cohesion is the result of intercommunication of specific ideas between the members of the social group. The ideas are transmissible visually and orally, by radio and television, newspapers or magazines, books, exhibitions, Internet, and so on. These ideas are from the "third world," as it was considered by Popper (1973); they are stored in library shelf space, nowadays in electronic space, and even in people's minds. They form the "sociocultural niche" associated with the social group.

3.2 EVIDENCES AND MEMES

The social niche is characterized by systems of ideas self-sustained in a complex with a given lifetime and which can be replaced by another complex of ideas. We shall distinguish two categories of ideas (Purica, 1988):

> The first category contains the ideas that can be experimentally verified. Their value is given, at least partially, not only by their acceptance by a social group, but this acceptance depends on the experimental possibility to attribute a truth-value as a result of verification in reality. We shall call such ideas "evidences," because to justify them we need evidence. Evidences are not only ideas from natural sciences or from social sciences but also from financial and economic systems, from technological systems, etc.
> The second category consists of self-sufficient ideas, that is, ideas called by Hofstadter (1983) "virus like sentences," or by Dawkins' (1976), with a more representative term, "memes."

A meme is defined by Dawkins in the *Selfish Gene* (1976):

"Examples of memes are tunes, ideas, catch phrases, clothes, fashions, ways of making pots or of building arches. Just as genes propagate themselves in the gene pool by leaping from body to body via sperms and eggs, so memes propagate themselves in the meme pool by leaping from brain to brain via a process, which, in the broad sense, can be called imitation (mimicking). If a scientist hears, or reads, about a good idea, he passes it on to his colleagues and students. He mentions it in his articles and his lectures. If the idea catches on, it can be said to propagate itself spreading from brain to brain."

When one plants a fertile meme in somebody's mind it is actually parasitizing that somebody's brain, turning it into a vehicle for the meme's propagation in just the same way that a virus may parasitize the genetic mechanism of a host cell.

Memes can evolve and, to do that, they have the three needed requisites—variation, selection, and heredity—of what Dennett calls the process: the evolutionary algorithm. It is a mindless procedure that produces "Design out of Chaos without the aid of Mind" (Dennett, 1995, p. 50).

The evolutionary algorithm depends on an entity that can be copied, and Dawkins, as we have seen above, calls this the meme.

A meme can therefore be defined as a unit of information that is copied with variations, and whose nature influences its own probability of replication (Dawkins, 1976).

One may also think of it as information that undergoes the evolutionary algorithm (Dennett, 1995) or as an entity that passes on its structure largely intact in successive replications (Hull, 1988) or information that is subject to blind variation with selective retention (Campbell, 1960).

Susan Blackmore (2001) introduces the idea of a discontinuous evolution of memes by identifying "a definite turning point—the advent of true imitation which created a new replicator," that is, the memes. She also suggests that there is a strategy for success, that is, "success is largely a matter of being able to acquire the currently important memes. So this strategy amounts to copying the best imitators. I shall call these people meme fountains, a term suggested by Dennett (pers. commun., 1998) to refer to those who are especially good at imitation and who therefore provide a plentiful source of memes—both old memes they have copied and new memes they have invented by building on, or combining, the old."

We would keep in our terminology the notion of cultural niche stemming from Popper that seems to be a more suggestive and general name for the concept. The important thing is, though, that Blackmore has coined the process of old and new memes that interact among them.

A meme is an idea, which results from an imitation accepted by a human intelligence. We must remember that even the ideas whose value is given by the interaction of man–nature or man–society, called "evidences," are transmitted partially by imitation. The teaching without the living of primary experiences is such an example. But the evidences may be exposed to an external proof of truth-value.

We consider the cultural niche as "open" in respect to evidences and "closed" in respect to memes, because the memes do not need any process to prove their truth. The truth of memes is a question of blind faith (confidence, credibility), which can justify anything.

In this context creativity means to accept the evidence and to transform it into new memes. This is in fact the deliverance from the "slavery" imposed by traditional memes specific to a cultural niche.

Creativity is a revolutionary act against the traditional memes, accepted as a result of education or entrenched corporate culture. This revolt appears by an accumulation of evidences formulated in the language. For example (Purica, 1989), at the beginning of the nineteenth century, when the honorable engineers designed naval industry of the wind ships, few scientists investigated the possibility to use the steam force. When the honorable engineers invented the steam engines there were few original scientists investigating the electrical and magnetic phenomena. When, at the beginning of the twentieth century the honorable engineers devised the electrotechnical engines, few curiosity-driven scientists experimented with nuclear radiation and today, when the honorable engineers are developing the nuclear power stations, there are few bizarre scientists dealing with possibilities offered by supergravity.

Other examples are possible to give, coming from the financial world related to the evolution from typical loans to project finance, to bonds, to derivative instruments, to various types of innovative financial instruments applied to such domains as dot.com, housing, etc.

The best way to put this evolution would be the formulation by the anthropologist Max Gluckmann: "... a science is any discipline in which the fool of this generation can go beyond the point reached by the genius of the last generation."

3.3 CREATIVITY AS A MEMES MUTATION

A nonspecified domain, which becomes a discipline, has a proper lifetime and this is sustained by a filiation of curiosity-driven persons. They need a specific sociocultural niche.

But the memes, like the genes, are susceptible of variation analogous to the mutations. Creativity may be described as a meme mutation imposed by a new evidence as a result of an experimental and theoretical effort to devise the new instruments.

We shall try to correlate the appearance of new ideas, of the "evidence" produced in the creative act, with the social dimension of creativity. The social group gives the utility value to the new meme, resulted by mutation.

Creativity implies, also, to convince the others to use what you have thought or done. It may be considered as a meme mutation with the same chance to be accepted by the social system. The initial set of evidences becomes a complex of memes, which evolves being accepted by the social group members of the cultural niche. We may consider the social dimension of creativity by a model describing the conversion of the social group members to a meme's complex resulting from a creative act.

The creative act initiates the appearance of evidences which, being able to propagate in the cultural niche, interact with the existing memes and transform them into different ones. The new memes, generated from evidence, are easily accepted by the members of the social group.

We shall represent the generation of new memes (N) by the evidence (E) as follows:

$$E \xrightarrow{I(E)} N \tag{3.1}$$

This is the first process of diffusion of the creative act. We will call this process "initiation."

The new memes, N, transform other memes, M, existing in the social group into N memes, compatible with the evidences:

$$M + N \underset{\lambda}{\overset{k}{\longleftrightarrow}} 2N \tag{3.2}$$

We note with k the rate of the transformation, as given in the representation of chemical reactions. The number of memes, N, generated in the time interval dt, by the interaction between a number, N, of new memes and traditional memes, M, in the cultural niche will be $kNM\,dt$.

We shall call such a process a "chain growth."

The inverse process by which the new memes are transformed into traditional memes with the rate λ, a process called "traditional involution," will decrease the number N by $\lambda N^2\,dt$.

The last process we will consider is the "assimilation" of the new meme, N, that cannot survive the comparison process with an old meme, C, and, thus, is transformed into a meme P, already existing in the cultural niche:

$$N + C \xrightarrow{\theta} P + C \tag{3.3}$$

The disappearance by assimilation of new memes, in a time dt, will be: $\theta NC\,dt$.

The four processes, initiation, chain growth, traditional involution, and assimilation, are the factors characteristic to the social dimension of the creativity propagation in the sociocultural niche.

We are interested in how the new memes, N, resulting from the creative act, evolve in the cultural niche.

The increase rate of the new memes $N(t)$ will take place with the rate $dN(t)/dt$:

$$dN(t)/dt = I(E) + (kM - \theta C)N - \lambda N^2 \qquad (3.4)$$

In a first approximation we consider that the cultural niche has a great number of memes, M, favorable to the chain growth and a constant number of C memes. We denote:

$$T = kM \quad \text{and} \quad T_c = \theta C \qquad (3.5)$$

The parameters T and T_c are characteristic for the sociocultural niche. They can be used to investigate the manner in which a creative act that has initiated the memes N may arrive to be dominant in the cultural niche. The factor T is specific for the acceptance of the N memes while T_c is specific for the conservative attitude.

We may use the terminology of Walls (1976) to describe the cultural niche temperature, T, and the critical temperature, T_c, using an analogy with the second-order phase transition. If the critical temperature is fixed, we can compare different cultural niches having different temperatures, T, that is, different numbers of memes, M, able to be converted by chain growth from the creative evidences $I(E)$. The steady states in the sociocultural niche will be given by the solution of the Eq. (3.4) where we put $dN(t)/dt = 0$.

As $I(E)$ may be a small term in comparison with the other two terms, we shall have the approximate steady state solutions:

$$\text{If } T < T_c; N_0 = 0 \qquad (3.6)$$

$$\text{If } T > T_c; N_1 = (T - T_c)/\lambda \qquad (3.7)$$

Thus, for a value of the temperature less than the critical temperature, the creative act remains without a social echo. We can denote the value T_c as being an "explosive limit" because if the temperature of the sociocultural niche surpasses T_c we have a rapid proliferation of the new meme.

The term "explosive limit" was used by Nicolis and Progogine (1977) to characterize chemical reactions, described by equations similar to (3.4).

If we reconsider the Eq. (3.4) without neglecting $I(E)$ for the steady state situation we have to look for the solutions of the equation:

$$N = K/(1 - (1 - K/N_0) \cdot \exp(-rt))N^2 - ((T - T_c)/\lambda)N - I(E)/\lambda = 0 \qquad (3.8)$$

This expression may be simplified to:

$$x^2 - a = 0 \qquad (3.9)$$

If we put:

$$x = N - (T - T_c)/\lambda \text{ and } a = ((T - T_c)/2\lambda)^2 + I(E)/\lambda \qquad (3.10)$$

We are faced with a fold catastrophe, in the language of the French topologist Rene Thom (1975), having only one singularity at $x = 0$. When $I(E)$ is small, such that: $I(E) \ll (T - T_c)^2/4\lambda^2$, and we approximate V_a by a series, the solutions for N will be:

$$\begin{array}{ll} T < T_c; & N_0 = -I(E)/(T - T_c) \\ T > T_c; & N_1 = ((T - T_c)/\lambda)[1 + I(E)\lambda/(T - T_c)] \end{array} \qquad (3.11)$$

We see in Figure 3.1 that excepting the neighborhood of the point T_c when N_0 and N_1 become infinities, justifying the term "explosive" used for the point T_c, the solutions (3.11) approach the solutions (3.7) when $I(E)$ is small.

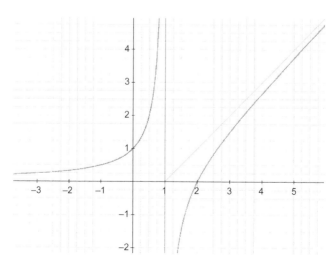

Figure 3.1 The solutions N(T) of Eq. (3.10) given by Eq. (3.11).

The condition that a result of a creative act leading to the mutation of a meme M into a meme N (concordant with the evidence E) will be imposed in a sociocultural niche will be:

$$T > T_c \text{ or } kM > \theta C \qquad (3.12)$$

We obtained the main result that the condition to impose a new meme in a sociocultural niche supposes the existence of a number of memes, M, transformable by chain growth with a rate, k, and a number of catalytic memes, C, which can assimilate the new memes, N, with a rate θ:

$$C/M < k/\theta \qquad (3.13)$$

The mathematical model proposed for the proliferation of a new meme in a sociocultural niche allows us to characterize the social dimensions of the creativity, as a dimension sustained with insistence by Taylor (1975) and Guilford (1972).

We can conclude that the social dimension may be specified if we consider a creative act as an initiation of a mutation of memes justified by one or more evidences.

3.4 LOGISTIC PENETRATION OF MEMES

We have seen in the previous section that the generation and penetration of memes in a cultural niche may be modeled with a reaction diffusion system that, in its simplest form, generates phase transition-like behavior.

Memes dynamic is described by an ordinary differential equation having a term in N^2 and a term in N (in the case when we have neglected the number of evidences that generate new memes as being small compared to the existing transformable memes in the niche).

Let us now analyze the dynamics of the differential equation of new memes penetration. We keep the previous notations.

The resulting equation is:

$$dN(t)/dt = I(E) + (kM - \theta C)N - \lambda N^2 \qquad (3.14)$$

and if we neglect $I(E)$ the equation becomes:

$$dN(t)/dt = (kM - \theta C)N - \lambda N^2 \qquad (3.15)$$

Rewriting the equation in a more adequate form we get the typical logistic equation first analyzed by Verhulst in the nineteenth century:

$$dN(t)/dt = (kM - \theta C)N \cdot (1 - N/((kM - \theta C)/\lambda))$$

where we note:

$r = (kM - \theta C)$; or with the previous chapter notation $(T - T_c)$, $K = ((kM - \theta C)/\lambda)$ as the N_{max}, that is, the carrying capacity limit of the logistic curve.

The logistic equation becomes:

$$dN/dt = rN(1 - N/K)$$

that has the well-known solution:

$$N = K/(1 - (1 - K/N_0) \cdot \exp(-rt))$$

or written differently as:

$$N = KN_0\exp(rt)/(K + N_0(\exp(rt) - 1))$$

with $N_0 = N(t = 0)$.

An important result of the above approach to the way new memes penetrate the cultural niche is the fact that this penetration is described by a logistic equation having the sigmoid curve as a solution.

One may recognize in the evolution of this solution the typical behavior of a new instrument penetration in the financial entity's cultural niche that has a slow beginning and, if successful, $(T > T_c)$ becomes dominant in the niche, generating a concentrated behavior toward using that instrument much more than others.

The logistic penetration process was extensively analyzed by International Institute for Applied Systems Analysis (IIASA) in relation to technologies and their cultural niches in various economic domains. Marchetti and Nakicenovic, as well as others, have presented the technique applied to various technologies such as energy conversion, transport, etc.

In one of his papers, Marchetti actually talks about credit taking from the banks, without getting into much detail though.

One of the things to notice in describing the logistic penetration relates to the fact that the new instrument penetration is measured as the ratio of new, F, to the rest of the niche $(1 - F)$, in percentages, such that the graph of penetration is actually showing the moments of each new instrument becoming dominant then decaying to let another instrument take its place. This description that is giving the $F/(1 - F)$ as an exponential function serves both in determining the values of r and K, from linear regression of $\ln(F/(1 - F))$, and it will also be used when we shall describe the decision process to allocate money to various financial instruments.

Let us analyze an example from the point of view of logistic behavior of the system. Consider the evolution of the financial instruments used in the USA during the crisis cycle of 2007. We should mention that when talking about the crisis cycle of a given year, for example, 2007, we refer to the period preceding that year, in which the logistic penetration took place and reached the saturation phase that triggered the discontinuous decision to abandon financing that instrument—a decision that is usually associated to a crisis.

A case analysis done by Barnett-Hart (2009) describes in great detail the evolution of collateralized debt obligations (CDOs) that, the author says, has been responsible for $542 billion in write-downs at financial institutions since the beginning of the credit crisis. The empirical analysis is based on extensive data on CDOs and, in light of our comments above, a figure draws attention. It depicts the evolution of the CDOs compared with other financial instruments (Figure 3.2).

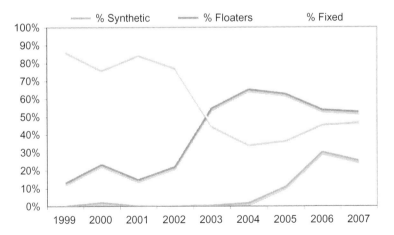

Figure 3.2 Historical changes in CDO bond collateral. Lehman Live.

3.4.1 Collateral Composition Trends in CDOs

Figure 3.2 shows the historical changes in CDO bond collateral among fixed rate, floating rate, and synthetic bond types.

To understand the recent implosion of the CDO market, it is helpful, as Barnett-Hart suggests, to examine the factors that fueled the market's explosive growth since 2004, as illustrated in Figure 3.3. There are two main factors that made the pooling and tranching of loans so attractive to the investors and investment banks that created CDOs—regulatory capital relief and risk reallocation.

Figure 3.3 is a typical example of a crisis cycle having an exponential growth phase in the first years and decaying abruptly at the end when the decision not to allocate money to CDOs was taken by the financial decision makers. Later on this type of evolution will be represented by the trajectory, in the decision space, that goes on one fold of the cusp, corresponding to the dominant instrument (CDO in this case), until it crosses the limit associated to the decision to abandon allocation of resources to this instrument. The evolution of the trajectory is dependent on the control parameters related to risk and to

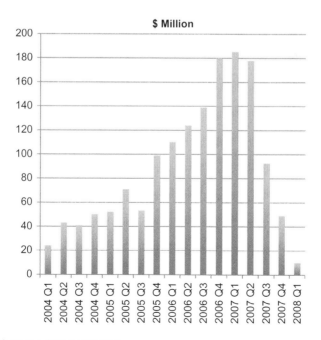

Figure 3.3 CDO issuance. Asset-Backed Alert.

benefits. What has been happening in the case under analysis is the increase of risk that was done in "creative ways" as further described.

Securitization helped many banks to free up their balance sheets, allowing them to pool and tranche a bundle of loans and either sell the tranches to outside investors or put them in off-balance sheet vehicles. By removing loans from their books, underwriters of CDOs could decrease the capital charges imposed by the Basel Accords and their own internal risk requirements and thereby free up cash to make new loans. Basel I required that banks hold capital of at least 8% of their loans. Basel II modified this slightly by imposing different charges based on the riskiness of the asset, often determined by the assets' credit ratings. See Garcia et al. (2008) for a more detailed explanation of capital requirement calculations. As we have mentioned, the risk monitoring is of great importance since it is a parameter that controls the distance to the limit of discontinuous decisions in the cusp many-fold space. All the elements described in relation to CDOs are actually connected to various forms of risk management.

The second rationale for CDOs involved the pooling and realloca-tion of risk. In theory, by pooling together a number of imperfectly correlated assets, it is possible to use diversification to decrease idio-syncratic risk. Furthermore, tranching the cash flows made it possible to create securities with different risk profiles appropriate to specific investors. Krahnen and Wilde (2005) finds that the senior tranches bear the highest degree of systematic risk, and Gibson (2004) shows that most of the credit risk is contained in the equity tranche, regard-less of the size of its notional amount.

This was especially important for institutional investors, many of whom can purchase only investment-grade securities (defined as those with a credit rating of BBB or higher). CDOs allowed these investors to gain exposure to assets that, on their own, had been too risky, while investors looking to take more risk and receive potentially higher returns could buy the most junior or "equity" CDO tranches. According to Lehman Brother's estimates, as of November 13, 2007, the biggest holders of AAA-rated CDO tranches included bond insurers, insurance companies, CDO commercial paper put providers, SIV (structured investment vehicle) and asset-backed commercial paper, conduits, and investment banks. As seen above, some elements of risk management are influencing the potential increase of benefits for institutional investors. This is taking us to the other parameter that controls the decision trajectory, that is, benefits. Because there is inter-dependence between these parameters the folds of the cusp are actually having a superposed flow of trajectories resulting from considering the system of differential equations associated with the variable and the parameters. This is discussed in detail later on.

Continuing with benefits identified by Barnett-Hart, it is seen that initially it seemed that every player was benefiting from CDOs and issuance exploded, reaching $50 billion in 2006. The rating agencies were making record profits as the demand for rated structured pro-ducts skyrocketed. Institutional investors loved the high-yielding AAA securities created from asset-backed security (ABS) CDOs, CDO underwriters collected fees and achieved regulatory capital relief by off-loading their assets, and CDO collateral managers earned hefty returns by retaining the equity tranches, benefiting from the low cost of funding senior tranches.

The actions taken, by 2003, to increase benefits have created the conditions for a small change to trigger a typhoon unleashed upon financial markets in 2007—just to use the butterfly effect metaphor.

First, the collateral composition of CDOs changed as collateral managers looked for ways to earn higher yields. The managers began investing more heavily in structured finance securities, most notably subprime residential mortgage-backed securities, as opposed to corpo-rate bonds.

Moreover, they invested in the mezzanine tranches of these securi-ties, moves designed to create higher-yielding collateral pools.

In addition to the increased investment in risky mortgage collateral, the next development was the creation of the notorious "CDO squared" (and the occasional "CDO cubed"), which repackaged the hard-to-sell mezzanine CDO tranches to create more AAA bonds for institutional investors.

Finally, the advent of synthetic CDOs significantly altered the evo-lution of the CDO market. Rather than investing in cash bonds, syn-thetic CDOs were created from pools of credit-default swap (CDS) contracts, essentially insurance contracts protecting against default of specific ABSs.

The use of CDS could give the same payoff profile as cash bonds, but did not require the upfront funding of buying a cash bond. Furthermore, using CDS as opposed to cash bonds gave CDO managers the freedom to securitize any bond without the need to locate, purchase, or own it prior to issuance.

Taken together, these observations indicate that CDOs began to invest in more risky assets over time, especially in subprime floating rate assets. Essentially, CDOs became a dumping ground for bonds that could not be sold on their own—bonds now referred to as "toxic waste." Quoting from Barnett-Hart: As former Goldman Sachs CMBS surveillance expert Mike Blum explains: Wall Street reaped huge profits from "creating filet mignon AAAs out of BB manure." In the IMF, Global Financial Stability Report "Containing Systemic Risks and Restoring Financial Soundness," April 2008, a detailed explanation is given to this process.

With the issuance of CDOs growing unabated and the quality of their collateral declining, both the rating agencies and the investment banks failed to recognize the amount of risk inherent in these products. Actually, in a meme interpretation, the traditional memes (determining T_c) that could have contributed to keep risk at an acceptable level were becoming a minority compared to the new memes, N, (that determine T) thus, ($T \gg T_c$ meaning a large r) generated a large-scale penetration of the meme associated to the specific financial instrument. This screened for a time any considerations of prudence. But, let us not forget that logistic penetration has two phases, a first exponential growth one and a second one of saturation. Regardless of our wishes, the second phase will eventually arrive and, with it, the discontinuous change perceived as crisis. There are ways to avoid the shock of change or to be prepared for it that will be discussed later.

Let us see how this dynamic is translated in the logistic penetration of the famous (now) subprime instruments.

REFERENCES

Barnett-Hart, A.K., 2009. The Story of the CDO Market Meltdown: An Empirical Analysis. Harvard College, Cambridge, MA.

Blackmore, S., 2001. Evolution and memes: the human brain as a selective imitation device. Cybern. Syst. 32 (1), 225–255, Taylor and Francis, Philadelphia, PA.

Campbell, D.T., 1960. Blind variation and selective retention in creative thought as in other knowledge processes. Psychol. Rev. 67, 380–400.

Dawkins, R., 1976. The Selfish Gene. Oxford University Press, Oxford (new edition with additional material, 1989, 30 years anniversary edition, 2006).

Dennett, D., 1995. Darwin's Dangerous Idea. Penguin, London.

Garcia, J., Goossens, S., Lamont, J., 2008. Dynamic Credit Portfolio Management: Linking Credit Risk Systems, Securitization and Standardized Credit Indices. SSRN Electronic Journal 01/2008; http://dx.doi.org/10.2139/ssrn.1274774.

Gibson, M.S., 2004. Understanding the Risk of Synthetic CDOs. Federal Reserve Board: Division of Research and Statistics, July 2004.

Guilford, J.B., 1972. La Creativite, in La Creativite, Recherches Americaines, Presente par Alain Beaudot. Dunod, Paris, pp. 9–27.

Hofstadter, D.R., 1983. Virus-like sentences and self-replicating structures. Scientific American, January 1983, p. 14.

Hull, D.L., 1988. Interactors versus vehicles. In: Plotkin, H.C. (Ed.), The Role of Behaviour in Evolution. MIT Press, Cambridge, MA.

Krahnen, J.P., Wilde, C., 2005. Risk Transfer with CDOs. Goethe-University, March 15, 2005.

Nicolis, G., Progogine, I., 1977. Self-Organisation in Nonequilibrium Systems. Wiley, London.

Popper, K., 1973. La Logique de la Decouverte Scientifique. Payot, France.

Purica, I., 1988. Creativity, intelligence and synergetic processes in the development of science. Scientometrics 13 (1–2), 11–24.

Purica, I., 1989. Creativity and the socio-cultural niche. Scientometrics 15 (3–4), 181–187.

Taylor, I.A., 1975. In: Taylor, I.A., Getels, T.W. (Eds.), Emerging Views of Creative Action, in Perspectives in Creativity. Aldine Publishing Company, Chicago, IL.

Thom, R., 1975. Structural Stability and Morphogenesis. N.A. Benjamin Inc., London.

Walls, D.F., 1976. Non-equilibrium phase transition in sociology. Collect. Phenom. 2, 125.

CHAPTER 4

Occupy the Financial Niche—Saturation and Crisis

This chapter introduces a model for the decision to allocate money to financial instruments, which is based on the logistic penetration of the associated memes. A Fokker–Planck equation is generated based on the resulting transition probabilities from the logistic behavior that makes the model similar to the Ising one in physics. The stationary solution of the Fokker–Planck equation shows bifurcation-like behavior that allows describing the evolution of decisions as trajectories on a "cusp" catastrophe folded surface controlled by such parameters as risk and benefits. Discontinuous decisions may thus be described such as abandon allocating money to a given instrument.

4.1 INTRODUCTION

The model presented is a theoretical approach within a broader research program that could verify the nonlinear conjectures made, such that to quantify and predict potential discontinuous behavior. In this case, the crisis behavior associated with financial funds reallocation among various credit instruments, described as memes with the sense of Dawkins, is shown to be of discontinuous nature stemming from a logistic penetration in the behavior niche. Actually, the logistic penetration is typical in creating cyclic behavior of economic structures as shown by Marchetti and others from the International Institute for Applied Systems Analysis (IIASA). A Fokker–Planck equation description results in a stationary solution having a bifurcation-like solution with evolution trajectories on a "cusp" type catastrophe that may describe discontinuous decision behavior.

4.2 SOCIAL REALITY AND COLLECTIVE BEHAVIOR

In a paper from the 1980s, Marchetti was identifying the spread out of ideas (e.g., technological innovation) as possessing biological properties such as mutation, selection, and diffusion. He was concentrating on the most obvious of the three mechanisms, that is, diffusion, identifying logistic penetration, and waves of economic behavior in different domains such as energy, innovation, transport, etc. In parallel, as we described above, Dawkins has developed the notion of meme as a concept that presents biological properties such as reaction, diffusion, mutation, and selection.

Sometime into the crisis unfolding, in 2009, I was reading an article by Jeffrey Sachs, in *Scientific American*, where the text below drew my attention:

> *There is little doubt that unduly large swings in macroeconomic policies have been a major contributor to our current crisis. During the decade from 1995 to 2005, then Federal Reserve chairman Alan Greenspan overreacted to several shocks to the economy. When financial turbulence hit in 1997 and 1998—the Asian crisis, the Russian rouble collapse and the failure of Long-Term Capital Management—the Fed increased liquidity and accidentally helped to set off the dot-com bubble. The Fed eased further in 1999 in anticipation of the illusory Y2K computer threat. When it subsequently tightened credit in 2000 and the dot-com bubble burst, the Fed quickly turned around and lowered interest rates again. The liquidity expansion was greatly amplified following 9/11, when the Fed cut interest rates sharply (eventually to a low of 1 per cent in June 2003) and thereby helped to set off the housing bubble, which has now collapsed.*

It occurred to me that several credit memes with the sense of Dawkins are penetrating the niche of the credit portfolio evolving in a logistic way, that is, slowly at the beginning, then bursting to finally saturate. The decision to allocate credit to the new penetrating credit meme may be described by a Fokker–Planck equation whose stationary solution is showing bifurcation behavior. This model may present the discontinuous decision to abandon a certain type of credit and allocate the money to the rest of the portfolio. The parameters driving this decision are: cost of risk (potentially measured by, e.g., spread or volatility) and benefit (measured by, e.g., yield).

In a collectivity, individual beliefs, desires, and decisions triggering actions are correlated into collective ones.

General sets of social facts may have subsets of institutional facts that result from a collective assignment of functions, which may be performed not only in virtue of their physical nature but also in virtue of their social acceptance by the collectivity as having a status assigned to them.

As an example, the noise made by a judge knocking at the end of a trial, without a definite status of behavior assigned to it, would only represent a natural noise. Conversely, taken inside the set of function-memes associated with the legal institution, the mentioned noise acquires a special meaning in terms of behavior.

Thus, in order for memes to have action value that ensures the forming of an institutional structure, a number of reactions need to happen with ideas and functions (described below as memes) that spread among individuals in a collectivity. This creates deontic powers such as rights, duties, obligations, permissions, and requirements. Not all of these are only institutional but without them, institutions would not exist as stable dynamic structures (Searle, 2005).

By creating institutional reality, human power is increased by its extended capacity for action. But the possibility to fulfill desires within the institutional structures (like getting rich in an economical structure or becoming president in a political structure) is based only on the recognition, acknowledgment, and acceptance of the deontic relationships.

The above statements require a basic intellectual cohesion that connects the members of a collectivity. This involves language as well as the media.

4.3 DYNAMICS OF MEMES

The movement of ideas and principles among the members of a collectivity creates a dynamic where sociocultural niches are formed as described by Popper (1973). To look deeper into the dynamic we will consider the memes introduced by Dawkins (the "virus-like sentences," in Douglas Hofstadter's terminology) that describe the basic conceptual framework for such an analysis (Purica, 1988).

There exists a certain intercorrelation of memes in a society that reacts and diffuses among the individuals. If looking at the financial world one may see it meets the typical criteria described above for a niche where the various financial instruments coexist as financial memes and have a specific dynamic. In what follows, we will analyze the way financial memes penetrate and occupy the niche.

We must underline that the fact that a given meme is having a larger part of the niche (call it financial market) depends of the perception by the decision makers of the potential advantage of the associated financial instrument. Moreover, it is important to stress that the decision to extend the use of a given instrument is based on perception that feeds from the creation of a collective effect.

The penetration of new financial instruments is done slowly at the beginning and then accelerated, to saturate toward the end. This is typically described by a logistic function. One may notice that this type of behavior has been shown to describe technology penetration in niches associated to technologies. Marchetti and Nakicenovic (1978), as well as other researchers from IIASA in Laxenburg have extensively done research on the logistic penetration of technologies with important results on the process understanding. Moreover, logistic penetration has been used to assess the saturation point of Internet networks or cell phones' market penetration.

As an example, a well-known figure is given below concerning the logistic penetration of energy technologies (Figure 4.1).

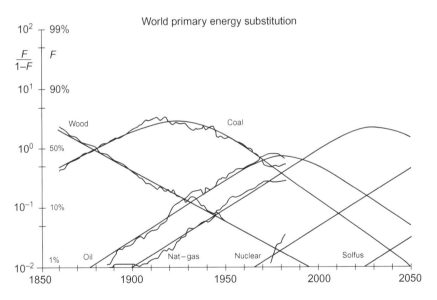

Figure 4.1 If the rate of introduction of newcomers in a niche compares with the time constants of the substitutions, we may have any number of competitors present at the same time, some phasing in and some phasing out. The great complexity of the process can be dealt with simple rules, reducing it to a one-to-one competition. Here the dynamics of the primary energy market at world level is represented in terms of market shares (in tons of coal equivalents!). The model fits snugly the statistics, in spite of the long time spanned and tribulated history. Nakicenovic, IIASA (1984).

Quoting Marchetti: "At this point it may be clear that the idea of an informational structure, after being created (mutation) and tested on the outside world (selection), will start diffusing. All the dynamic of the system can then be reduced to a sequence of diffusion processes in a highly hierarchical set of niches. The fact that diffusion proceeds with great stability and that when new competitors will start diffusing, the rules of the game are always the same, gives the possibility of using this methodology for precision forecasting. Basically, the rules are very simple. The successful newcomer penetrates logistically, i.e. takes increasing shares of the niche, following a logistic equation. Old losers phase out logistically. One competitor in between takes what is left from these rigid courses" (Marchetti, 1986).

We may note that Marchetti is making an attempt to analyze the evolution of credit taking from banks that identifies some features of the same behavior, but without identifying the general cause of such behavior, which is related to decision makers' behavior in relation to the decision to allocate money to various financial instruments counted as portfolio of financial institutions. This is where we are bringing some added value in introducing the memes as defined above and the Fokker–Planck equation approach (see also Purica, 1991, 2013).

The logistic behavior is perceived in the case of financial instruments as moments of crisis, when a given instrument after having occupied a large portion of the market (niche) saturates, that is, falls fast.

The data from the 1998 crisis and from the 2007 one (just to take the last two) were showing the same type of behavior obviously in relation to different instruments. As we have shown in the beginning of our analysis it seems there are periods of repeated penetration and decrease of some financial meme. See Figure 4.2 below.

A typical logistic behavior is seen in the niche of financial instruments used, described as memes, showing increase in the sum allocated to some instruments as they occupy larger parts of the financial market to diminish after saturation and switching to other financial memes.

Let us go back to subprimes now and see their position in the allocation of assets evolution in the US during 1999–2007. This is given in Table 4.1 below that summarizes the average collateral composition of 742 security asset-backed collateralized debt obligation (CDO) deals originated between 1999 and 2007.

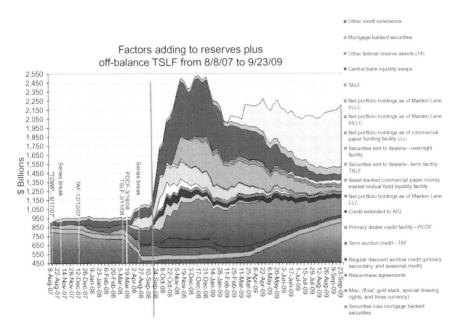

Figure 4.2 Evolution of various financial instruments in 2007–2008. IAES Conference, Boston, October 2009.

Table 4.1 Average Principal Allocations by Asset-Class

Year Originating	Deals	REL	RSMB	CSMB	CDO	OSAB
1999	1	0%	14%	9%	3%	74%
2000	16	5%	1%	2%	12%	80%
2001	28	7%	6%	8%	18%	61%
2002	47	16%	6%	7%	8%	63%
2003	44	29%	14%	3%	18%	37%
2004	101	35%	14%	6%	17%	28%
2005	153	37%	16%	10%	11%	25%
2006	217	33%	16%	7%	9%	35%
2007	135	36%	12%	8%	14%	29%

The abbreviations stand for: REL   residential equity loan (includes all RSMB less than prime), RSMB residential securities mortgage-backed (by prime borrowers), CSMB   commercial securities mortgage-backed, OSAB   other securities asset-backed (including auto loans, credit cards, etc.).
Source: *Lehman Live.*

One thing to mention is that we have purposefully slightly changed the names of the instruments from the usual literature ones. This is done specifically to make the reader get out of the interpretation reflexes created by seeing the same names and pay more attention to the fact that more information is taken out of the same data by using

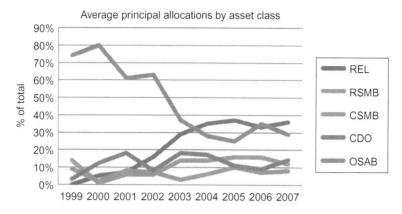

Figure 4.3 Average principal allocations by asset class. Author calculations based on Lehman Live data in Table 4.1.

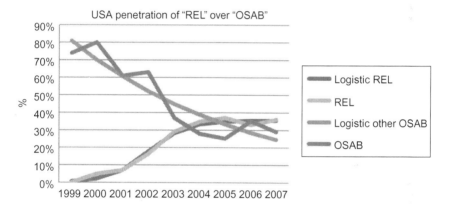

Figure 4.4 USA penetration of "REL" over "OSAB". Author calculations based on Lehman Live data.

the approach we describe here. It is in fact a question of memes perception that we try to change.

The evolution of the allocations in Table 4.1 is also shown in Figure 4.3.

We are concentrating now on the REL—representing the subprimes. One may see that the evolution in this niche of financial instruments shows a typical case as described above, of logistic penetration of an instrument, REL, to the detriment of another, previously dominant one, OSAB.

Figure 4.4 represents the two instruments and the respective logistic functions resulting from a logistic regression on the two sets of data.

The set of logistic function is presented below:

For REL:

$$\text{Logistic REL}$$
$$a = 263.5$$
$$b = 1.388$$
$$c = 0.3554$$
$$\text{REL} = c/(1 + a \times \exp(-b \times x))$$

For OSAB:

$$\text{Logistic OSAB}$$
$$a = 8.11$$
$$b = -0.158$$
$$c = 8.5$$
$$\text{OSAB} = c/(1 + a \times \exp(-b \times x))$$

As seen from the description of the logistic penetration we have here a case of a slow start at the beginning, then it is fast, followed by saturation, penetration of a new financial instrument in the financial niche. This follows a "sigmoid" curve and takes the niche away from the previous dominant instrument that decays, also following a logistic curve. It is a process described by Marchetti, Nakicenovic, and Pry, as well as others who have studied this type of process in various domains (niches).

We have shown in our analysis that the process of logistic penetration is actually also happening in the niche of financial instruments that is at the basis of financial systems' operation.

But in the world of today, planning the development of financial systems means having to take into account a large and intricate pattern of various indicators not only connected with economical aspects, but also with the political, sociological, environmental, etc.

The good fitting of the statistical data by the logistic function is only providing the financial planner with a method to predict the evolution of financial instruments' penetration in the future. It does not show how to change and control such an evolution. So, it represents just an experimental assertion, a very important and necessary one, but not a consistent theory, which would provide the criteria and the means for deciding and influencing the evolution of financial systems.

We are trying to provide a means to fill this gap by analyzing the case of funds allocation, measured in monetary units, for the intensification of one or the other of two financial instruments in competition, with the imposed or wished variations of the external parameters represented by indicators of benefits and costs of risk control. This way, development decisions may be taken to avoid sudden, unprepared, and large discontinuities, resulting in impacts that may affect the evolution of the financial programs.

4.4 DESCRIPTION OF THE MODEL

We shall now review the main ideas that have led to the construction of the model; for a more detailed presentation the reader is referred to Gheorghe and Purica (1979), Gheorghe and Purica (1982), Ursu et al. (1985), and Purica (2010).

4.4.1 Experimental Grounds

In order to understand the notion of transfer probability in the model we come back to a paper of 1971 where Fisher and Pry (1971) tried to fit the statistical data with two-parameter logistic functions of the type:

$$F/(1 - F) = \exp(at + b) \tag{4.1}$$

where

t is the independent variable measuring the time,
a and b are the coefficients of the logistic curves,
F is the portion of the technological market occupied by the new technologies, and
$(1 - F)$ is the portion occupied by the old technologies.

This paper together with Peterka (1977) was the base for Marchetti and Peterka, who extended the logistic penetration model to more than two technologies. Since we have seen that the same function may be applied for financial instruments, we think a thorough datamining program should be launched as a basis for a research program on the evolution of various financial niches—associated with financial entities—such as to be in a position to determine the transition probabilities of the model that follows.

The basic supposition that we extend to memes states that if the substitution of an old instrument with a new one takes place, then the process continues following a logistic curve.

Extending this to a decision level we analyze the decision to intensify one or the other of two financial instruments in competition by transferring monetary funds between their development programs. The possibility to predict the result of abandoning the funding of one of the programs is thus opened up, among others, to the decision maker.

The competition between financial instruments in each moment of time is described by a distribution function of the probability to have, at that moment, a certain partition function of the total fund between the two instruments development programs.

The distribution function is the stationary solution of a Fokker–Planck equation whose form depends on the expression of the transition probabilities associated with the decision of transferring funds between the two financial instruments.

If we consider that the replacement of an instrument by another is the result of a fund transfer decision from one instrument to the other one, we notice that $F/(1 - F)$ represents the frequency of occurrence of the event of partial replacement of an instrument by the other.

At the limit we may associate with the decision a transition probability expressed as an exponential function (associated to the expression of $F/(1 - F)$). So, our model is in close resemblance to the Ising model in physics, also used for the description of the polarization of opinion processes in sociology.

Within this approach the coefficients I and B, used in the expression of the transition probabilities, have precise meanings, their variation (given or imposed) determining the system's behavior.

4.4.2 The Master Equation of the Process

We start by admitting that the structure of an economy's financial system may be described as a collection of financial instruments weighted by a given distribution.

In terms relevant to decision making, the weight of a given instrument or group of financial instruments may be measured by the amount of money put at each moment, t, into the development and deployment of that particular instrument.

For the sake of simplicity we assume that

the total amount of money, M, allocated to the financial niche is
practically constant within the observation time lapse;
we consider only two types of financial instruments, although one
may also consider one instrument and the rest of the niche.

So, we may write

$$M = M_1 + M_2 \qquad (4.2)$$

with M_i, $i = 1$, 2 being the allocated funds for the two types of
instruments.

Intensifying, for example, the type-one instrument is represented by
the transition $(M_1, M_2) \rightarrow (M_1 + 1, M_2 - 1)$.

The decision process leading to an allocation is stochastic and cooperative since a given decision is the result of a complex interaction of memes
among individuals and/or groups, sensitive to their respective monetary
power of influence of each of them, in terms of sound arguments, number,
effectiveness, etc., and to external circumstances like market, policy, etc.

That is why one is interested in describing the probability distribution
function, f, to have, at a moment, t, decided on an allocation (M_1, M_2).

In order to find it, we write the master equation of this process:

$$f(M_1, M_2, t)/t = w_{21}(M_1 + 1, M_2 - 1) \cdot f(M_1 + 1, M_2 - 1, t)$$
$$+ w_{12}(M_1 - 1, M_2 + 1) \cdot f(M_1 - 1, M_2 + 1, t) \qquad (4.3)$$
$$- (w_{21}(M_1, M_2) + w_{12}(M_1, M_2)) \cdot f(M_1, M_2, t)$$

which represents the balance between entering the state (M_1, M_2) from
and leaving it for, the neighboring states $(M_1 - 1, M_2 + 1)$ and
$(M_1 + 1, M_2 - 1)$; see Figure 4.5.

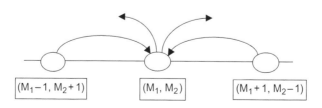

Figure 4.5 Funds allocation. Done by the author.

w_{21} and w_{12} are dependent on the probabilities per unit time of the transitions $1 \rightarrow 2$ and $2 \rightarrow 1$, respectively. They are obviously proportional to the effective amount of money in the initial state and must also account for the cooperative character of the decision process underlining transitions.

As we have seen above, the transition probabilities are of exponential form. By similarity to the Ising model in physics we may say that the chance of a $1 \rightarrow 2$ transition is enhanced by options already made in favor of the second kind of instruments while discouraged by options already made in favor of the first kind of instruments. The opposite goes for a $2 \rightarrow 1$ transition.

With these assumptions w_{12} and w_{21} read:

$$w_{12}(M_1, M_2) = M_1/M \, \exp[-(1/\theta) \cdot (I \cdot (M_1/M - M_2/M)/2 + B)]$$
$$w_{21}(M_1, M_2) = M_2/M \, \exp[+(1/\theta) \cdot (I \cdot (M_1/M - M_2/M)/2 + B)]$$
$$(4.4)$$

4.4.3 Identification of the System Variable and Control Parameters

The parameter I is a measure of the intensity of the financial system; that is, proportional to the benefits, B is a "preference parameter" accounting for external influences on the decision process, that is, proportional to risks, and θ is a "decision climate" parameter: the higher the θ is, the higher the temperature of the debate, owing to a higher perception of the crisis.

Choosing the specific indicators for I and B, in the case of financial instruments, must take into account both the integrative character of these indicators and the scale of magnitude of the financial instruments domain under investigation.

For example, when describing the interplay of two categories of financial instruments one should choose the indicators from the set of financial indicators related to a specific niche that could be just a bank or a national financial system.

In order to solve the master Eq. (4.3) we define for large M the continuous variable:

$$x = (M_1/M - M_2/M)/2 \qquad (4.5)$$

From (4.5) and (4.2) we have:

$$M_1/M = 1/2 + x$$
$$M_2/M = 1/2 - x \tag{4.6}$$

Expanding all functions of x up to the second order in $1/M$, one gets a Fokker–Planck-type equation:

$$df/dt = -dJ/dx \tag{4.7}$$

where the current J is given by

$$J(x) = 1/M \cdot (w_{21} - w_{12})f - 1/(2M)^2 \cdot d/dx \cdot ((w_{21} + w_{12})f) \tag{4.8}$$

The stationary solution ($J = 0$) is found to be

$$f(x) = \text{const} \cdot [1/M \cdot (w_{21}(x) + w_{12}(x))]^{-1} \exp[2M] \\ \times \int_{-1/2}^{x} dx'[(w_{21}(x') - w_{12}(x'))/(w_{21}(x') + w_{12}(x'))] \tag{4.9}$$

where:

$$w_{12}(x) = (1/2 + x)\exp(-1/\theta \cdot (I \cdot x + B))$$
$$w_{21}(x) = (1/2 + x)\exp(1/\theta \cdot (I \cdot x + B))$$

4.4.4 Change of Stationary Solution with Variations of the Control Parameters—the "Cusp" Type Catastrophe

A numerical analysis of f given by Haken (1981, pp. 340–341) for $B = 0$ and various I/θ shows some remarkable features (see Figure 4.6).

Writing the formula with $f(x) = y$ and $I/\theta = n$ and scaling such that to have a graph around zero, we obtain the various distributions, for specific values of n, where the shape goes from a single minimum to two, showing a bifurcation pattern specific to the cusp catastrophe of Rene Thom.

$$y = \left(\frac{1}{\cos h(nx) - 2x \sin h(nx)}\right) e^{\left(0.01 \int_{-0.5}^{x} (\sin h(nt) - 2x \cos h(nt)/\cos h(nt) - 2x \sin h(nt))dt\right)}$$

On a different scale for x and for y ($1.5 - y$) (values are chosen to illustrate the trend; calculations for the case of the 2007 crisis are done later in the book) one may see that as I/θ increases, the one maximum (stable point) at $x = 0$ bifurcates into two maximums at $x < 0$ and $x > 0$.

1. It says essentially that the higher the financial intensity of a given economy, the higher the chances that strong stands can be taken for more than one financial option;

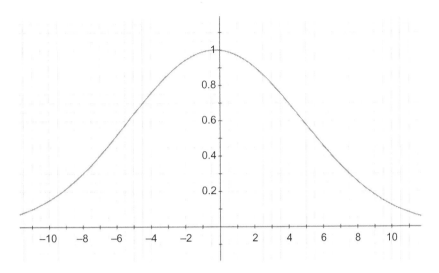

Figure 4.6 Stationary solution behavior case $I/\theta = 0$.

2. subsequently, that clear decisions are to be expected (sharp probability peaks) when the decision climate is favorable (θ is small, i.e.,
the "temperature of the debates" is kept low).

Letting $u = I/\theta$ and $v = B/\theta$, the function f becomes $f(x, u, v)$.

Watching the bifurcation in Figures 4.6–4.10, we may, along with
Thom (1972), admit that this shape of the function f implies the existence in the space (x, u, v) of a topological surface of the points corresponding to the extreme states of the function f. This surface
corresponds to the "cusp" type catastrophe. Because its points represent the extremes of the function f, which are the equilibrium states of
the system, the evolution of the system may be represented by trajectories on this topological surface (see Figure 4.11).

As it was shown by Thom, this topological surface is determined by
a potential whose derivative has the form:

$$dV(x, u, v)/dx = x^3 + u \cdot x + v \tag{4.10}$$

The projection of the topological surface in Figure 4.11 on the
plane (u, v) is a characteristic bifurcation whose branches represent the
limit when a small variation of the parameters implies a sudden change
of the system's state, that is, a sudden large reallocation of funds
between the two financial instruments.

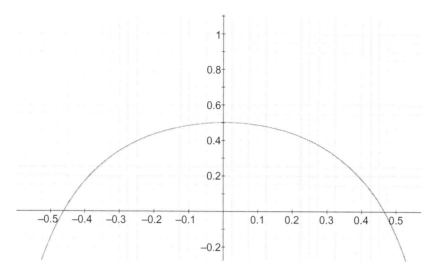

Figure 4.7 Stationary solution behavior case 1/θ = 0.5.

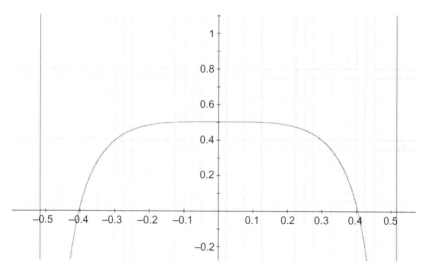

Figure 4.8 Stationary solution behavior case 1/θ = 2.

We said above that u is a parameter for the intensity of the financial instrument and in what follows we take it as measured by the benefits of that instrument, while v is a "preference parameter," which we measure by the costs of risk control. We have thus established the control parameters.

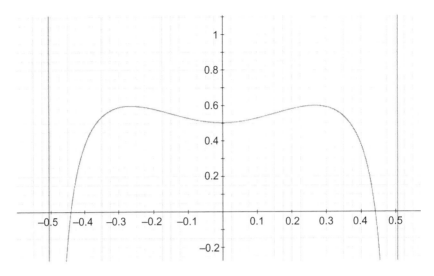

Figure 4.9 Stationary solution behavior case 1/θ = 2.5.

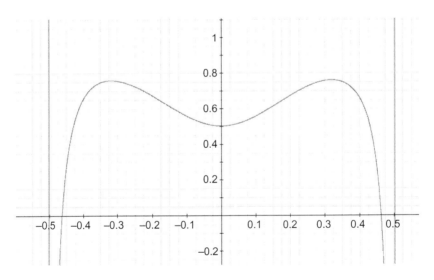

Figure 4.10 Stationary solution behavior case 1/θ = 3. Done by the author based on Haken (1981).

First we note that we can no longer consider the control parameters u and v as independent.

Finding a certain dynamic dependence between the parameters also implies the fast variable x imposes a flow of trajectories on the smooth surface of the cusp.

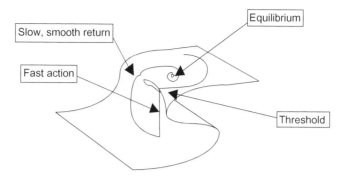

Figure 4.11 A flow of trajectories on the cusp fold potential crisis behavior. Done by the author.

The dynamic equations resulting from the interdependence of x, u, and v are given below for a qualitative example based on the interplay between x, u, and v.

We first consider that the time variation (x') of the fast variable is proportional to dV/dx; V being the potential corresponding to the cusp catastrophe. In a meme interpretation we believe more in something, which we have already supported with money and previous trust.

Then we take the variation of the benefits (u') as proportional to the value of the benefit and to the value of the funds allocated to the instrument. In memes language we tend to favor the instruments that bring more benefits and those in which we have put more money.

The variation of the costs of risk control (v') depends on the benefits obtained, from which a constant value v_0 is subtracted, defined as the limit value of the costs of risk control that makes the instruments acceptable to the niche, for example, society. Here the memes favor either the instruments that bring more benefit for more risk, or the ones that bring benefit for less risk—the transfer of risk for various types of instruments that resulted in reduction of the cost of risk going under the level of acceptance v_0.

The dynamical system we obtain reads:

$$x' = -(x^3 + x \cdot u + v)$$
$$u' = a \cdot u + bx \qquad (4.11)$$
$$v' = c \cdot u - v_0$$

Figure 4.11 shows the flow of trajectories on the topological surface.

We see that the equilibrium is given, putting $x' = u' = v' = 0$, and is the point of the coordinates:

$$x_e = (av_0)/(bc)$$
$$u_e = v_0/c \qquad\qquad (4.12)$$
$$v_e = -(av_0^2)/(bc^2) \cdot ((a/b)^2(v_0/c) - 1)$$

The branches of the cusp are given by:

$$4 \cdot u^3 + 27 \cdot v^2 = 0 \qquad\qquad (4.13)$$

From Figure 4.11 we see that by raising v (costs of risk control), we reach a critical value when a large reallocation of funds to a different type of instruments is necessary.

The critical border is not crossed if the benefits of the first instruments are increased by, for example, finding new applications for it that are of interest to the society.

If we consider a, b, and c as constants, we see that the equilibrium points (x_e, u_e, v_e) depend on v_0, which is the measure of a society's acceptance of an instrument from the point of view of its cost of risk control.

The example above assumes a linear dependence on u and v.

Even in this rather simple case, it results in a strong dependence of the planner's decision on the society's perception of level of risk (v_0).

It is important to mention that in the above conditions, the equilibrium point is a stable one that all evolution trajectories converge toward one another. The critical points give an indication of the path to equilibrium, which may be either smooth or discontinuous if the trajectory is crossing from one fold to another. As long as the trajectories remain close enough to the equilibrium point, this one is perceived as stable (convergent), but taking more risk than a given limit (increased cost of risk control) throws the trajectories over the limit of perceived stability into a discontinuous change to abandon allocation of funds to the dominant financial instrument.

The above behavior is a potential qualitative explanation of the pre-crisis perception that nothing may go wrong. With a linear approach the equilibrium point seems stable, meaning that all trajectories converge to it.

In reality, though, there are limits that once crossed do not allow a smooth return in a short time. The available choices range from long-time smooth returns to a second discontinuity that may be untenable for the system's resilience (meant as capability to absorb shocks).

The findings by Reinhard and Rogoff in terms of the perception that "this time is different" relate to a "negative" type of meme that creates the collective behavior associated to the refusal, until the last moment, to believe the existence of limits that may be crossed eventually.

We are still slaves of a linear type of mental thinking; especially when things seem to go well, acknowledging the existence of limits is the last thing one accepts to do. On this line, we stress again that in ancient Rome, when a victorious general was having a triumph and was hailed by the crowds, there was in his chariot a man telling him, "remember you are mortal." It seems we have lost this sense of limits.

4.5 CRITERIA FOR FINANCIAL DEVELOPMENT STRATEGIES

4.5.1 Beyond Resilience—Decisions for Safety

Going through the cases described above, we have seen that each sudden jump from one fold to the other means a large reallocation of funds between the two financial instruments. Every such reallocation represents an effort, which must be made by that specific institution (even that nation) changing the evolution strategy of its financial systems.

The question arises of what are the amplitude and frequencies of such shock-like efforts, which the nation's economy can still absorb and sustain without being completely perturbed.

We have here the very definition of resilience as given by Haefele (1977). But our model goes beyond that by first being able to discern between the amplitudes of shocks and their frequencies of occurrence, thus giving a limit on amplitude—transferred funds—a limit on frequency, and a limit on the total number of shocks. When any of these are reached, the economy is drastically perturbed.

By extending the mechanical analogy we may define a fatigue limit, measured by the number of cyclic shocks (funds reallocation) an economy can sustain before becoming completely exhausted and being forced to change its whole development in order to recover. This would be represented as a series of successive hysteresis-like cycles in the evolution of the decision trajectory.

Combined amplitude and frequency effects of shocks may be accommodated within our model.

Another feature of this approach is the possibility to predict the arrival of shocks and, based on their predicted amplitude, to decide the most appropriate variations of the control parameters in order to avoid the shock or to mitigate its consequences if it is accepted.

Being able to make such decisions gives the financial system's planner the possibility to optimize the social effort for financial development, thus contributing to an increase in the nation's economic, social, and ecological safety.

4.5.2 Perception of Alternatives and Strategic Conduct

To summarize: through a variety of paths, financial decision makers will probably strive toward a status of maximum financial security, or even "over security" taking advantage of their increased margins of resilience as their financial activity increases.

All paths would, in principle, require timely adjustments in the financial infrastructure of the economy. The amplitude of the adjustment varies with the financial condition of an economy and with the kind of path chosen. If the need for adjustment is ignored, some paths, when followed persistently and blindly, can drive the financial system and the economy into critical states of disruption.

Faced with these findings, it is clear that a prompt and correct perception of the need and the size of structural adjustments in the financial system is a prerequisite for a sound and smooth financial policy.

In terms of this approach, long-term planning of the financial systems means, among other things:

i. forecasting where one's path is to enter the critical area of the cusp, since, at that moment, the development of potential alternatives to the established financial infrastructure becomes both possible and increasingly advisable;

ii. forecasting where the respective resilience limit is in order to avoid crossing it through current swings in policy, which may prove costly and painful for society.

Such a generic strategy, advocating R&D programs in principle with not much of an apparent short-term market justification, might have a number of unappealing features. While ignoring the market reality and indulging in wishful thinking is certainly risky, a nonanticipative, noncreative attitude toward the market looks equally unadvisable, for there is also a risk with being too late in giving the green light to latent, sound alternatives that take some unforgiving lead time to develop.

On the other hand, it is only obvious that no need for crash programs exists when the financial evolution path is chosen appropriately, thus avoiding any accidental and unprepared crossing of the resilience borders of the financial system.

While there is a cost and risk to any change, the fact that there is also a cost and risk to ignoring the need for changes seems inescapable. An attitude that treats alternatives not only as subversions of the existing establishment, but also as safeguards of its stability and also generators of future, ever more appropriate patterns, is of great importance for both the planner and the public.

REFERENCES

Fisher, J.C., Pry, R.H., 1971. A Simple Substitution Model of Technological Change. Report 70-C-215. General Electric Company, Research and Development Center, Schenectady, NY.

Gheorghe, A., Purica, I., 1979. Decision Behaviour in Energy Development Program. University of Bucharest, Division of System Study, The University Press, Bucharest.

Gheorghe, A., Purica, I., 1982. The decision behavior in energy development programmes. Found. Control. Eng. 7 (2).

Haefele, W., 1977. On Energy Demand. IAEA General Conference, Vienna.

Haken, H., 1981. Synergetics, Introduction. Springer Verlag, Berlin.

Marchetti, C., Stable Rules in Social and Economic Behaviour, Lecture held at the Brazilian Academy of Sciences, November 11, 1986.

Marchetti, C., Nakicenovic, N., 1978. The Dynamics of Energy Systems and the Logistic Substitution Model. IIASA AR-78-18.

Peterka, V., 1977. Macro-dynamics of Technological Change: Market Penetration by New Technologies. IIASA RR-11-22.

Popper, K., 1973. La logique de la decouverte scientifique. Payot, France.

Purica, I., 1988. Creativity, intelligence and synergetic processes in the development of science. Scientometrics 13 (1−2), 11−24.

Purica, I., 1991. Synergetic application of complex ordered processes. In: Maino, G. (Ed.), Proceedings of ENEA Workshops on Non-linear Systems, vol. 3. Simulation of Non-linear Systems in Physics. World Scientific Publishing, Singapore.

Purica, I., 2010. Nonlinear Models for Economic Decision Processes. Imperial College Press, London, ISBN:9781848164277.

Purica, I., 2013. Occupy the financial niche: saturation and crisis. In: Stavrinides, S.G., et al. (Eds.), Chaos and Complex Systems. Springer Verlag, Berlin, pp. 125−130. Available from: http://dx.doi.org/10.107/9783642339141_16.

Searle, J.R., 2005. What is an institution? J. Inst. Econ. 1 (1), 1−22.

Thom, R., 1972. Stabilite Structurelle et Morphogenese. W.A. Benjamin, Inc., Advanced Book Program, Reading, MA.

Ursu, I., Purica, I., et al., 1985. Socio-economic risk in development of energy systems. Risk. Anal. 5 (4).

CHAPTER 5

Monitoring Issues and Measuring the Change

This chapter uses the derivative of the logistic function to identify the change from exponential growth to saturation in a logistic curve as a predictor of the occurrence of saturation that will trigger a discontinuous decision. Further on it calculates the example of the subprime instruments' evolution in the decision folded space and identifies the cross-point of the limit of decision change to abandon financing them. A procedure for crisis prediction is also proposed.

5.1 PREDICT THE PHASE CHANGE

One element that regulatory entities and associated rating ones are asked to provide is prediction of the change. The approach we have taken here uses concepts that are based on the existence of limits—either limits imposed by a given carrying capacity of a logistic curve or limits given by the folded spaces of catastrophe theory.

These limits are giving the possibility to predict when they are approached by the evolution trajectory of a system, or when they will be crossed by that trajectory. To be fully aware of this capacity of prediction one may have to start thinking in terms of trends occurring in dynamic second-order nonlinear systems (at least) where the notion of equilibrium is the exception and not the rule of normal behavior.

For example, let us come back to the case of residential equity loan (REL) (subprime) instruments penetration from 1999 till 2007 that, as we have seen, was following a logistic curve. The characteristic of such a curve is given by the change in the derivative of the function. The first "exponential growth" part of the curve has an increasing derivative while the change to the "saturation" part is producing a decrease in the derivative as seen in Figure 5.1A and B.

Looking at the data for REL derivative (actually resulting from the logistic equation) one may see that the change from increase to decrease is taking place around 2002–2003. This could be a sign that

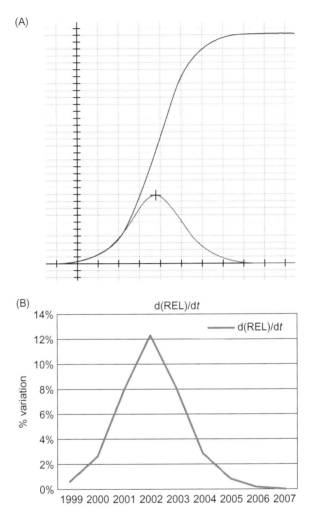

Figure 5.1 (A) Logistic curve and its derivative, qualitative behavior. (B) Derivative of the logistic curve, data for 1999–2007 REL. Author's calculations.

the saturation phase has started and there would be ample time to prepare for taking the appropriate decisions either to avoid the saturation—that implies to avoid a discontinuous decision associated to a crisis—or to prepare absorbing the impact, if the system is resilient enough.

Another way to verify this result is to calculate the time coordinate of the inflexion point of the logistic function (i.e., change from "exponential growth" to saturation). The time coordinate is resulting from the logistic function formula as $t = \ln(a)/b$, with the notation of the logistic function parameters from the previous chapter. The resulting value is $t = \ln$

(263.5)/1.388 = 4.016 years. Since we have started in 1999, the year of the saturation start is 2002–2003. The value of the market penetration at this moment in time is $c/2$, which is 0.3554/2 = 0.1777, that is, 17.77%.

The calculation of the moment of saturation start was made based on the parameters determined for the logistic regression done on the data after the process had ended. In order to monitor the change during the process one should rely on the derivative of the logistic function. This implies that at least 1 year (or whatever time disaggregation unit is used) must pass after the change of trend is seen. This may still leave enough time to prepare the necessary decisions to avoid or adsorb the discontinuous shock.

Having a dedicated entity that monitors the penetration of various financial instruments and assesses periodically the status of the dominant instrument and its derivative, change of trend may provide a good prediction for the occurrence of crisis situations.

We are ending this example with the conclusion that the financial instruments are designed to evolve exponentially in a world that has limits and acts in a logistic way. If the time constants are small one may confound the purely exponential evolution with the "exponential growth" of the logistic curve. I will call that a Malthusian perception by contrast to the full deployment of the logistic curve (a Verhulstian perception) toward saturation and sudden change, based on discontinuous decisions.

5.2 CROSSING THE LIMIT IN THE DECISION SPACE

One step further in our examples is the value of $u = I/\theta$—the parameter in the transition probabilities that determined the size of the bifurcation of the stationary solution, that is, the position on the cusp-folded surface. The values calculated from the logistic representation of the transition probabilities, based on the REL data in Figure 4.4, give a value of $u = b/c = 3.9$. Figures 4.6–4.10 show that the bifurcation is increasing with $u = I/\theta$, and since the value of 3.9 is higher than 2.5 and 3 represented in the figure, the bifurcation is more pronounced. This means that the trajectory of the system is in a region where a discontinuous transition is possible if the amount of risk taking is increased over the specific critical value of the limit in that region of the decision space. Equation (4.13) in Chapter 4 allows the calculation of the limit curve value $v = \mathrm{SQRT}(4u^{\wedge}3/27) = 2.96$. The value of $v_r = \mathrm{POWER}(u^{\wedge}2/16 \times 27,1/3)$ associated to u on the decision trajectory is 2.95, which is a good indication that the evolution trajectory has gone beyond the limit requesting a discontinuous decision to abandon allocating money to this instrument. Figure 5.2 is showing this dynamic.

Figure 5.2 is another example where numbers that are having a meaning, given by a nonlinear model, may have a greater prediction capacity than the usual linear models we are accustomed with. Of course, the image of a decision trajectory controlled by benefits and cost of risk evolving in a space having various types of limits (possibly moving limits) that may or may not be crossed with associated consequences is a much better way to visualize this type of behavior.

A possible image of the trajectory evolution is given in Figure 5.3.

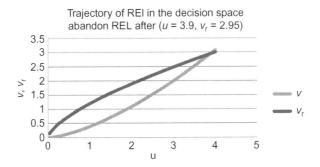

Figure 5.2 REL trajectory in the decision parameters' space. Author's calculations.

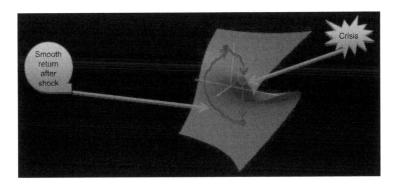

Figure 5.3 The cusp catastrophe, decision space. Done by the author.

Allow me to claim the copyright for such a possible computer game of financial reality that will actually be played mainly by CEOs of financial institutions.

5.3 CASES OF DECISION TRAJECTORY EVOLUTION

Having set up the conceptual framework for the nonlinear behavior of financial instruments' evolution, let us use it to describe some of the crisis-like periods that have happened in the last years.

A seminal paper by Semmler and Bernard (2012) is describing some of these cases that we will "translate" in relation to the concepts introduced above.

The synthesis they make of the observable behavior that leads to "boom—bust cycles" starts first with focusing on the assessment of risk and then on the perception of benefits.

Quoting from this paper: "Efficient capital markets are supposed to evaluate and price risk; but frequently, if risk assessment is measured and priced through financial market instruments, we observe significant non-robustness in risk evaluation and asset prices. Moreover, markets exhibit externalities, resulting in failures, disintermediation, and meltdowns. The busts, precipitated by financial instability, usually entail contagion effects and strong negative impacts for the real side of the economy."

The above is actually describing the reaction diffusion of memes that, in the Malthusian phase (exponential growth) of the cycle (the "boom"), leads to diminishing the perception of risks as a part of the new dominant meme initiating penetration. Later on the saturation phase (Verhulst phase) sets in and the existing risks (previously almost neglected) are perceived at a much higher value than they really have. This risk pricing, down/up, is marking firstly the beginning of the penetration of a new meme and secondly the saturation final phase. In this case each new financial instrument has a perception, given by the associated meme that makes the decision to allocate money to it, that is biased firstly toward more allocation and secondly toward withdrawal of funds. This discontinuous change is happening on the risk perception (pricing) side.

The merit of the authors, among other things, is to have identified a pattern of behavior associated to the "boom—bust" cycles.

Quoting again: "There is some synchronized behavior of economic agents and some mechanisms, observable in boom–bust cycles, that are rather general: the boom period triggers overconfidence, overvaluation of assets, over-leveraging, and the underestimation of risk; then follows a triggering event and the market mood turns pessimistic; finally, undervaluation of asset prices and deleveraging. Most of the historically experienced boom–bust cycles exhibited such features."

This time we see a full pattern of meme-driven phase transition-like process. If we are accustomed to water vaporization-condensation phase transitions and even devised ways to use it to our benefits based on Carnot and other types of thermodynamic cycles, the cyclic phase transition of financial markets is not yet fully understood. Maybe, in a hopefully not-so-distant future, we will be able to use these "boom–bust" cycles (actually phase transitions of memes reflected in financial decisions with impacts on the real economy) to convert "financial heat" into useful "economic energy" that will generate positive evolution.

The types of cycles we are discussing may be represented on a cusp-like folded surface like a succession of up/down going trajectory triggered by a succession of discontinuous decisions determined by memes penetration in a perception space associated to financial instruments allocation of money.

A possible representation may be similar to the evolution of technical discoveries (see Purica, 2010) that have a similar logistic-like evolution on the cusp manyfold as shown in Figure 5.4.

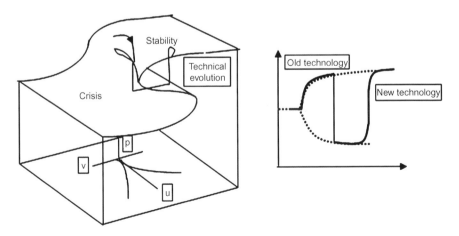

Figure 5.4 Evolution of new technologies penetration and saturation (the same boom–bust cycles, i.e., logistic-like behavior similar to the financial instruments). Purica (2010).

Going along with Semmler and Bernard we see that all the three examples of the latest crises, discussed in their paper, fit the pattern of evolution described above.

The emerging-markets crisis of the 1990s started with Mexico (1994), then went on with the Asian tigers (1997/1998), followed by Russia (1998), and Argentina (2001). The euphoric (specific memes penetration) state following capital market liberalization in those countries had generated a boom period characterized by the lowering of risk perceptions, overvaluation of asset prices foreign borrowing, and capital inflows. After the first phase was over, then when the second phase came suddenly, the distrust of the countries' basic lack of reforms led to a sudden reversal of these same capital flows; this triggered financial instability, rapid exchange-rate depreciation, and, consequently, a sharp decline in economic activity.

In those years the foreign direct investment (FDI) in emerging economies was about three times the government investment, and the fashionable meme was that the government should stay away from the economy that was powered by FDI. After the crisis took its toll the fashionable meme was that somebody should take the risk, perceived at overestimated price. Obviously, that somebody would be the government. This "Wall Street" versus "Main Street" balance of risk taking also showed up in the 2007 crisis. It is important to mention that till not so long ago the governments were considered as infinite reservoirs of risk absorption and, consequently, T-bonds were risk-free instruments. Recent years have shown that there is a carrying capacity of governments (see Greece lately) that comes to manifest itself if the risk taking or the amount of credits is over the given limits. Again, this is a manifestation of a logistic type of world and not an exponential one. Are we getting into phase two of the logistic penetration? Is this supposed to generate discontinuous decisions related to how money will be allocated and how monitoring of the process will be done? One sure thing is that we come to see that even in the financial world the behavior is still logistic, that is, there are limits to consider in deciding on future evolution.

Another crisis cycle to consider is the information technology (IT) of the 1990s. During the period 2001 till 2002, the financial markets have seen a significant decline in asset prices, referred to as the dot-com's of the IT stock market bubble. Lowering of risk perceptions along with overvaluation of asset prices, preceded by a decade of dubious accounting practices (see MacAvoy and Millstein, 2004) and unusual investment, led to a situation where, suddenly, equity valuations sharply declined.

The interesting thing coming out of these types of similar unfolding of the crises is the fashionable meme of the time. Every period of crisis is preceded by a euphoria of the universal solution of growth—remember the "information highways." One good solution for growth would be to sell as fast as you can before the "universal solution" meme reaches saturation and everything changes suddenly. Else, there is another fashion that somehow disappeared, that is, the one of jumping from skyscrapers after one loses everything.

The last crisis cycle is the recent financial meltdown, which began in the US subprime (mortgage) market in 2007 (actually as we have shown above the crisis second phase conditions had set in earlier). The evolution continued as credit crisis through the US-banking system in 2008/2009, and subsequently spread worldwide. This had caused a general financial panic and significant declines in global growth rates. As we have described above, the usual crisis cycle mechanism was triggered by new financial innovations; specifically, the development of new financial intermediations through complex securities, for example, mortgage-backed securities (MBSs), collateralized debt obligations (CDOs), and credit-default swaps (CDSs).

The thing to consider here is that the complex securities, which were actually trying to reduce risk perception, have actually accelerated the two phases of the cycle: the first phase through high asset prices and high leveraging and the second phase producing an asset—price collapse and credit crunch.

Those new instruments provided the magnification of a financial mechanism through which the asset price crisis cycle became more prominent. The present financial crisis is not fully analyzed. It seems to be neither a financial crisis triggered by a currency run nor a technology bubble, but rather a homemade financial crisis resulting from two driving forces: macroeconomic changes (financial market liberalization, low interest rates, high liquidity, easy credit, and external imbalance) and the use of new financial innovations and new tools of risk management, which substantially helped to increase leveraging.

We have analyzed above how the use of new financial instruments contributed in the first phase to create the crisis conditions with actually no monitoring to foresee the credibility-carrying capacity limit and then passed to the second saturation phase that generated discontinuous decisions that have changed the trajectory of evolution.

Semmler and Bernard (2012) are expressing the opinion that overall, they assume that there are nonlinearities, possibly giving rise to an asset price boom and then, maybe later on, to a bust. These nonlinearities are in fact present in the two phases the logistic penetration manifests itself, first with an exponential growth, later followed by saturation. These are what are correctly perceived as the boom and bust stages of the crisis cycle. They continue saying that the recently observed amplification of the expansion and contraction of leveraging is likely to be related to the way new financial instruments are employed, including the new financial tools that have accelerated the rapid buildup and contraction of credit, thus triggering the collapse in asset pricing.

In this context, the recent development of new financial instruments, in particular, credit derivatives and their use in securitization products, such as MBSs and CDOs, are of particular importance. These have allowed lenders to off-load risk and remove sensitivity to longer-term prospects. More specifically, by grouping large numbers of mortgages together, securitized instruments are created that are very nonrobust in performance; that is, small changes in interest rates, delinquency rates, recovery rates, and default correlations can lead to a collapse of security prices and to the bursting of the bubble. The description above is a typical representation of the evolution on the folded surface of a cusp-type catastrophe—as shown above—where the trajectory of decision on supporting the security price may change drastically upon small changes of the indicators that are integrated in the expression of the risk-related parameter. This type of behavior, as well as others related postcrisis recovery or precrisis prediction, may be accommodated in the representation of the logistic penetration of financial instruments that trigger decisions based on the memes associated with each instrument.

Continuing with the qualitative description developed by Semmler and Bernard we see they consider that there are two regions of attracting associated to risk premiums and to benefits such as profit expectations on assets values. The value of the risk premium may vary according to several integrated components while the value of the benefit is measured by asset pricing and leveraging. The sudden drop of asset prices as well as leveraging might have come, hint the authors, from the sensitivity of the pricing of complex securities with respect to small changes in delinquency rates, default correlations, and so on, and this might also explain the collapse of the Case–Shiller index.

This description is clearly supporting the approach taken in this book where the formalization is more extended and explanation of the discontinuous decision behavior is put in the context of a Fokker–Planck-equation approach leading to a decision space that has two folds and where passing from a fold to the other, that is, sudden change of the variable, is determined by small changes of control parameters. The approach we have taken allows the determination from real data of the evolution of the financial instruments penetration in their niche of the transition probabilities for the process and to make numerical predictions related to how close the trajectory is to the limit of sudden change. This puts the decision maker in the position to be prepared to avoid or take the shock of the discontinuous change.

5.4 FREEDOM VERSUS DEREGULATION—HISTORICAL CONSIDERATIONS

The seeds of financial liberalization and globalization boom phase of the crisis were introduced in the early 1980s by extensive deregulation of financial markets in the developed world, especially the Reagan administration reforms in the USA and the Thatcher administration reforms in the UK. The result in terms of perception was that operation on the full planet was similar to a system having no limits—we stress again there is no such thing as no limits but only the temporary meme of such a system existing that parasitizes the minds of people.

These actions were guided by belief systems and ideologies wishing to restore a more capitalist tradition, and they finally diffused across the global system. French President Mitterrand's attempt to advance a more socialist set of values and policies were overcome by late 1982, and financial market deregulation and international integration spread not only in Western Europe and North America, but also to Asia, Latin America, Africa, and Eastern Europe.

New unregulated financial products, entities, and markets came to play a larger role. Also, fast advances in information-processing technology (the computer revolution, electronic banking systems, communication satellites, etc.) facilitated international arbitrage. All this enhanced the perception that not only space but even time limits were remote since transactions decreased time constants substantially.

The commoditization and securitization of financial products by the private sector, including through virtually unregulated no-reserve-requirement "offshore banking facilities," led to dramatic increases in international money liquidity and credit, and by the end of the 1980s, global financial markets were generating a net international flow of funds of more than $3 trillion each month, that is, the flow of funds between countries that reconciles end of the month balance of payments accounts. Of that $3 trillion, $2 trillion was so-called stateless money, which was virtually beyond the control of any government or official institution, but available for use by all countries (Barron's Magazine, 1987, p. 45).

This 1980–2006 boom phase of the current crisis was driven by fundamental changes in the basic social and technical rules of the game, or "meso" structure of the global economy (as per the evolutionary economics language, Dopfer et al., 2004), which, among other characteristics, replaced more hierarchically organized, communitarian-disciplined, national-government-controlled rules with, instead, more free-market, technologically innovative, decentralized, and chaotically individualistic meso structures as financial globalism took over. We stress again that the ideas of rules that replicate and associate with meso structures in economic systems, together with the statement (Foster and Wild, 1999) that structural change may be indicated by logistic evolution, are a first conceptual step toward introducing more nonlinearity in the description of crisis evolution.

Allen (1999) shows that these structural changes associated with financial globalization supported an increasing net financial inflow from the rest of the world into the USA from near-balance in 1980 to approximately $800 billion per year or 6% of GDP as a net financial inflow in 2006—the peak of the long boom—which supported classic-pattern excesses in low-interest rate debt financing and spending, monetary wealth creation processes, consumerism and financial asset inflation, and now-famous lax standards in mortgage financing and securitization vehicles such as "CDOs" and "structured investment vehicles" that passed the rights to the mortgage payments and related credit/default risk to third-party investors. The US household personal savings rate dropped from 8% of disposable income to 0% over this 1980–2006 period, while the "net wealth of the US" (net value of business assets, real estate, consumer durables, and US government property) increased from approximately $7 trillion to $50 trillion in nominal terms.

During this period from the early 1980s to 2006, there were several crisis cycles occurring triggered by the same mechanism of a new financial instrument becoming dominant after an exponential growth period, followed by saturation and discontinuous change. The beginning of the 2007 crisis bust phase began with the burst of the US housing bubble and a sudden rise in home foreclosures in the USA in late 2006, which spread to become a more broad-based global financial crisis within a year.

Major banks and other financial institutions reported losses of approximately $100 billion by the end of 2007. By October 2007, 16% of subprime loans in the USA with variable interest rate features were 90 days delinquent or in foreclosure proceedings, roughly triple the rate of 2005, and by January of 2008, this number increased to 21%. Losses in the money-credit pyramid then began to spread across the system including through the collapse in June 2007 of two hedge funds owned by Bear Stearns that were invested heavily in subprime mortgages.

The lender-of-last-resort (LOLR) phase of the crisis began as the Federal Reserve took unprecedented steps to avoid a Bear Stearns bankruptcy by assuming $30 billion in its liabilities and engineering the sale of Bear Stearns to JPMorgan Chase. In August 2008 the US Treasury (and therefore the US taxpayer) joined the LOLR phase by taking over and guaranteeing the funding of Fannie Mae and Freddie Mac, the quasi-government housing market entities. In September 2008 American International Group, because of its exposure to CDSs, was bailed out by the Federal Reserve in an $85 billion deal, and then later that month the US taxpayer-sponsored $700 billion bailout bill was passed after Congress amended the plan to add more oversight, limits on executive pay, and the option for the government to gain equity in the companies that it bails out. As in Finland and Sweden's crises in 1991, Europe and the USA quickly moved to acquire equity stakes in, and partly nationalize, the banks.

The first reaction of the state entities is to return to "social market capitalism" control of the financial system of the pre-1980 rule structures that were more hierarchically organized and disciplined (by treasuries and central banks and other official institutions) in place of the more free-market innovative, decentralized, and individualistic rule structures that dominated between 1980 and 2008.

In testimony before the US Congress on October 23, 2008, former US Federal Reserve Chairman Alan Greenspan famously said that: "I made a mistake in presuming that the self-interest of organizations, specifically banks and others, was such that they were best capable of protecting their own shareholders."

5.5 PROCEDURE FOR PREDICTING CRISIS CYCLES

In light of the above dynamics we may determine some basic steps of the action to predict the crisis cycle.

The first would be to monitor the financial niches and the logistic penetration of financial instruments in order to find the dominant one.

Then, monitor the derivative of the dominant instrument evolution curve to identify the phase change moment from "exponential growth" to saturation.

Further on, draw the trajectory of the dominant instrument in the decision space by evaluating the values of the parameters and find its position with respect to the limit of discontinuous decision.

Following this, check evolution scenarios and the possibility to control the parameters such as to avoid crossing the limit or to determine when, that is, at what values of the parameters in their evolution, the limit will be crossed.

Now, one is in the position to prepare for adsorbing the shock in finance and in the economy, and design return strategies either as a hysteresis cycle or on a longer smooth path.

To some extent costs may be assessed for the avoidance of the shock or for the various associated return strategies in case the shock took place.

REFERENCES

Allen, R.E., 1999. Financial Crises and Recession in the Global Economy, second ed. Edward Elgar, Northampton, MA.

Barron's Magazine, 1987. The globalization of the industrialized economies. Barron's, May 4.

Dopfer, K., Foster, J., Potts, J., 2004. Micro, meso, macro. J. Evol. Econ. 14, 263–279.

Foster, J., Wild, P., 1999. Detecting self-organizational change in economic processes exhibiting logistic growth. J. Evol. Econ. 9, 109–133.

MacAvoy, P., Millstein, I., 2004. The Recurrent Crisis in Corporate Governance. Palgrave-Macmillan.

Purica, I., 2010. Nonlinear Models for Economic Decision Processes. Imperial College Press, London, ISBN: 9781848164277.

Semmler, W., Bernard, L., 2012. Boom-bust cycles: Leveraging, complex securities, and asset prices. J. Econ. Behav. Organ. 81 (2012), 442–465.

CHAPTER 6

Nonlinear Effects in Market Penetration—Deterministic Chaos

This chapter uses a second-order logistic map to show that the penetration of financial instruments may show various types of behavior ranging from decay to logistic penetration to chaotic (deterministic chaos). The specific coefficient calculated in previous chapters for subprimes is typical for chaotic behavior. An analysis is done with a view to understand this complex behavior.

Let us go along with Purica (2010) and apply the approach of a discrete logistic function, that is, a logistic map, to the processes described in previous chapters. Recent years have revealed the possibility of applying a number of newly found mathematical concepts like "deterministic chaos," "catastrophe theory," "bifurcation theory," etc., to the description of economic systems' behavior. These concepts have been proved to be more accurate descriptors of several types of nonlinear dynamic systems, thus arriving at the identification of certain specific mechanisms by which the outcome of complex, "chaotic" behavior may be predicted.

One such mechanism is shown to occur in the process of penetration of new financial instruments on a market dominated by an existing pattern of instruments.

Some comments on the rate of penetration and its role in producing chaotic evolution along with the role of the regulatory activity will follow.

6.1 QUADRATIC PHASE DIAGRAMS IN ECONOMICS

For a better understanding of the process, we give a few cases related to the way second-order dynamic relationships can arise in economics starting with a simple example (Baumol and Benhabib, 1989) showing this pattern. Consider the relationship between a firm's profits and its advertising budget decision. Suppose that without any expenditure on advertising, the firm cannot sell anything. As advertising outlay rises, total net profit first increases, then gradually levels off and finally begins to decline, yielding the traditional hill-shaped profit curve. If P_t represents total profit in period t and y_t is total advertising outlay, P_t can, for illustration, be expressed as $P_t = ay_t(l - y_t)$. If the firm devotes a fixed proportion, b, of its current profit to advertising outlays in the following period so that $y_{t+1} = bP_t$, the first equation is transformed into our basic chaos one with $w = ab$.

The reason the slope of the phase graph turns from positive to negative in this case is clear and widely recognized. Even if an increase in advertising outlay always raises total revenue, after a point its marginal net profit yield becomes negative and hence the phase diagram exhibits a hill-shaped curve.

Giving it some thought, one may see why the time path of y_t can be expected to be oscillatory. Suppose the initial level of advertising, y_o, is an intermediate one that yields a high-profit figure P_o. That will lead to a large (excessive) advertising outlay yl in the next period, thereby bringing down the value of profit figure P_1. That, in turn, will reduce advertising again and raise profit and so on *ad infinitum*.

The thing to be noted about this process is that it gives good reason to expect the time paths of profit and advertising expenditures to be oscillatory. But it does not give us any reason to expect that these time paths need either to be convergent or perfectly replicatory. This is an example of how chaotic behavior patterns can arise.

Another example has been provided in the theory of productivity growth (Baumol and Wolff, 1983). It involves the relationship between the rate of productivity growth (P_t) and the level of R&D expenditures by the private industry (r). Obviously, a rise in r can be expected to increase P_t. However, since research can be interpreted as a service activity with a more or less fixed labor component, its costs will be raised by productivity growth in the remainder of the economy and the resulting stimulus to real wages. This, in turn, will cut back the quantity of R&D demanded. The result, as a formal model easily confirms, is a cycle with high productivity rates leading to high R&D prices, which restrict the next period's productivity growth, and so reduce R&D prices and so on. If R&D costs ultimately increase disproportionately with increases in productivity growth, it is clear that the relation $P_{t+1} = f(P_t)$ can generate the sort of parabolic-shaped phase graph that is consistent with a chaotic regime.

Another model that can generate cyclic or chaotic dynamics is a standard growth model of Solow type in which the propensity to save out of wages is lower than that for profits. Suppose that at low levels of capital stock K one obtains increasing marginal returns to increased capital, and the elasticity of substitution of labor for capital is initially low, but diminishing returns eventually set in and the elasticity of substitution moves the other way. Then total profits can rise, at first, relative to total wages, but later profits may fall both relative to wages, and even absolutely. This can generate a hill-shaped relationship between K_{t+1} and K_t as rising K_t at first elicits rising savings and then eventually depresses them as profits fall.

6.2 PENETRATION OF A FINANCIAL INSTRUMENT

As we have seen in the previous chapters the penetration of a financial instrument is following a logistic curve in the niche of such instruments represented by financial entities. Let us now pass from a continuous description of the process to a discrete one where the logistic function is given by a second-order map described by:

$$x_{n+1} = rx_n(1 - x_n)$$

A description of the properties of such a map, done using Wolfram Alpha, is given in Appendix 2. One may see that the associated behavior ranges from decay to logistic penetration to oscillatory period doubling cycles to chaotic (deterministic chaos) behavior.

If we consider now the case we have calculated for the residential equity loans (RELs) and introduce the value of the obtained coefficient for $r = 3.9$ in the logistic recursive relation, we have that the penetration is chaotic (deterministic chaos behavior).

For comparison we give the cases when the coefficient is smaller than 1, between 1 and 2, between 2 and 3, between 3 and 4, and 4. It is seen that the behavior is changing in each case from decay to logistic penetration to oscillatory and finally to deterministic chaos. Calculating the coefficient of the map could represent a potential measure of the type of behavior expected to happen in the system.

Figures 6.1–6.6 describe various types of behavior that are generated with a rather simple formula. The approach taken here shows that a nonlinear type of function (such as a second-order logistic map) may bring the

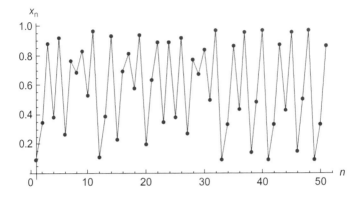

Figure 6.1 Chaotic regime for r = 3.9.

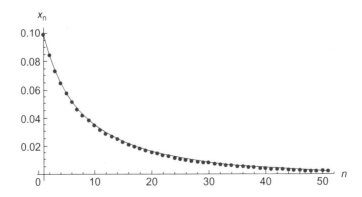

Figure 6.2 Regime for r < 1.

logistic map	
parameter r	1.368
initial condition x_0	0.1

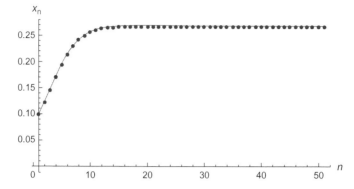

Figure 6.3 Regime for $1 < r < 2$.

logistic map	
parameter r	2.5
initial condition x_0	0.1

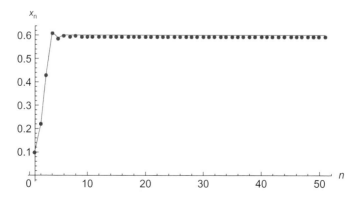

Figure 6.4 Regime for $2 < r < 3$.

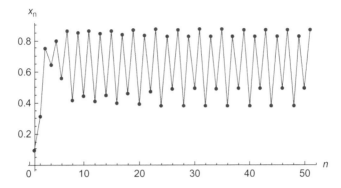

Figure 6.5 Regime for $3 < \mathrm{r} < 4$.

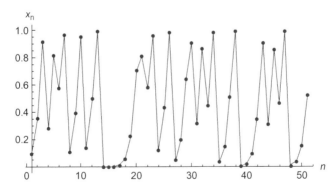

Figure 6.6 Regime for $\mathrm{r} = 4$.

process of penetration of the market by various financial instruments to a more predictive capacity resulting from the ability to model several types of behaviors depending on the values of a parameter—values that can be measured based on the data evolution of real cases.

An online monitoring of the data, associated with calculation of the specific parameters and with a representation of the decision trajectories' evolution related to the limits of no return, is possible to be done as a signal of potential danger of a discontinuous decision.

One must see the behavior as describing various potential evolutions:

i. $0 < r < 1$—the financial instrument is thrown out of the niche and its percentage of occupation decaying to zero in a given amount of time;

ii. $1 < r < 3$—the penetration is smooth following a logistic curve;

iii. $3 < r < 4$—the penetration is showing bifurcation of cycles and finally chaotic (deterministic chaos) behavior.

Let us consider that the characteristic total revenue (R_m) of a dominant instrument is another typical case of a parabolic-shaped process: at zero quantity demanded (Q) total revenue is zero at whatever price, while at a price of zero, R_m is zero although the quantity demanded could be positive. The slope of any line from the origin to the $R_m(Q)$ curve is the marginal price of the item at the corresponding output level.

If we consider now the penetration phase of the new instrument as taking place in a perfect competition market, it is obvious that the total revenue R_n will have a linear dependence on the quantity demanded.

The process of passing from the dominant instrument in the niche (market) to the perfect competition phase of the new instrument that penetrates the market is characterized by the shift of the total quantity demanded from the dominant instrument to quantities of the new instrument.

So, if at year y_t the dominant instrument occupies the market providing all the quantity demanded, it obtains a total revenue given by the parabolic equation:

$$R_m(Q) = m \cdot Q(1 - Q)$$

where Q is the ratio between the actual demand and the total potential demand of the economy.

Let us suppose that the next year, y_{t+1}, part of the demand Q (i.e., nQ) is provided from the new instrument, which gives a total perfect competition revenue $R_n = p \cdot (n \cdot Q)$, with p being the price of the new instrument. Thus, n is a measure of the rate of penetration of the new instrument in the niche.

Further on, we may consider that the new instrument (perfect competition) revenue $R_n(t + l)$ is proportional to the previous year's dominant instrument revenue $q \cdot R_m(t)$, where q is also an indication of the rate of penetration of the new instrument on the revenue side.

Resuming the suppositions above, one obtains:

$$R_m(t) = m \cdot Q(l - Q) \tag{6.1}$$

$$R_n(t) = p \cdot (n \cdot Q) \tag{6.2}$$

$$R_n(t + l) = q \cdot R_m(t) \tag{6.3}$$

From Eqs. (6.1) and (6.2) we have:

$$R_m(t) = m/(p \cdot n) \cdot R_n(t)(1 - R_n(t)/(p \cdot n)) \tag{6.4}$$

which, together with (6.3), gives:

$$R_n(t + l) = q \cdot m/(p \cdot n) \cdot R_n(t)(1 - R_n(t)/(p \cdot n)) \tag{6.5}$$

Relation (6.5) represents a typical process where "chaotic" behavior may occur as described above. In order to bring it to the canonical form we have, as a first alternative, to make the assumption that $p \cdot n = l$. This actually says that the share of the demand n, that the new instrument may hope to cover, is inversely proportional to the price p that it uses on the market, which represents a sensible conclusion.

We have that $(q \cdot m/(pn)) = r$ is the parameter we have discussed above regarding the outcome of chaos. Considering the limits emerging in the dynamics and focusing on the relation between the dominant instrument parameter m and the new instrument revenue rate of penetration parameter q, we have:

$qm < l$, which means the phase curve will lie below the 45° line in the first quadrant; and the process will show a tendency to extinction of the new instrument's revenue (Figure 6.7).

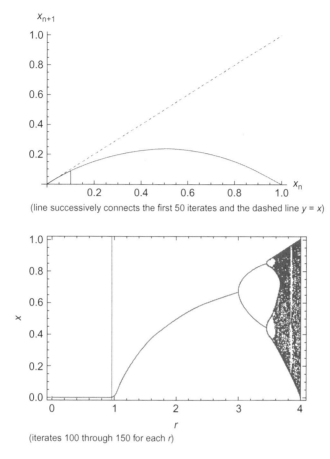

(line successively connects the first 50 iterates and the dashed line $y = x$)

(iterates 100 through 150 for each r)

Figure 6.7 Case qm < 1.

$1 < qm < 3$, which means there will be a positive value equilibrium point at the intersection of the $45°$ line and the parabolic curve; the new instrument revenue converges to it, as a stable state, a logistic curve going to the carrying capacity.

We may notice that:

$1 < qm < 2$ where the phase curve slope at the intersection point will be positive (Figure 6.8);

$2 < qm < 3$ where the slope will be negative but less than unity in absolute value (Figure 6.9);

$qm > 3$ where the slope will be less than -1; the new instrument revenue will start oscillating, first experiencing various doublings of the period then passing to a chaotic regime (Figures 6.10 and 6.11).

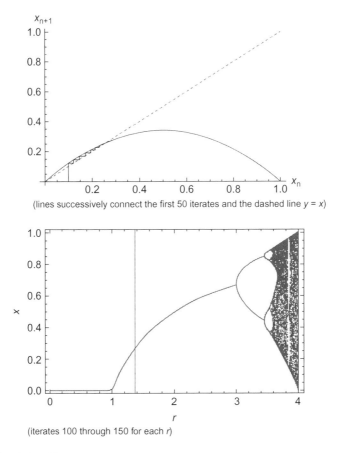

(lines successively connect the first 50 iterates and the dashed line $y = x$)

(iterates 100 through 150 for each r)

Figure 6.8 Case $1 < $ qm < 2.

Analyzing how this translates into considerations on the new instrument penetration rate q, it follows easily from the above inequalities that:

$q < (1/m)$ gives an extinction of the new instrument penetration, thus representing a lower limit of supporting the new instrument, below which it is inefficient to pursue it.

$(1/m) < q < (3/m)$ gives an interval where the new instrument revenue will converge to a stable value. Since this value will increase with the penetration parameter value going up, there is a strong tendency toward a fast penetration obtained with a strong support of the new instrument.

$(3/m) < q$, which means that, beyond this limit, the new instrument revenue starts oscillating, tending to a very complex ("chaotic")

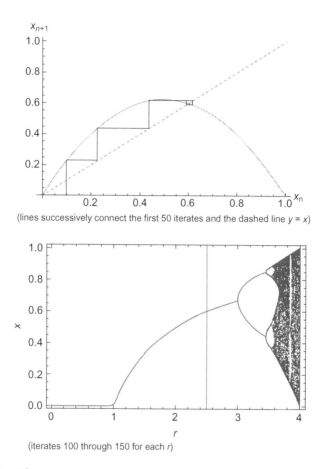

(lines successively connect the first 50 iterates and the dashed line $y = x$)

(iterates 100 through 150 for each r)

Figure 6.9 $2 < $ qm $ < 3$.

behavior, and is thus seemingly unpredictable implying a decision to discontinue its support.

If now we consider Eq. (6.5) and, instead of putting the condition $p \cdot n = 1$, we rescale R_n as $R = R_n/(pn)$, we obtain,

$$R = (q \cdot m/(p \cdot n)) \cdot R(1 - R) \qquad (6.6)$$

One important conclusion to draw here is that as the price of the new instrument decreases (e.g., subprime situation) the value of the parameter r increases leading to the range of chaotic behavior.

Finally we see that by considering the logistic discrete map we are in a position to describe various types of behaviors related to the

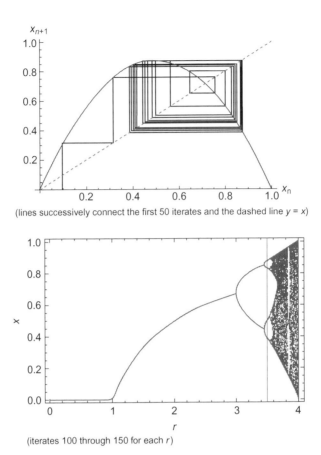

(lines successively connect the first 50 iterates and the dashed line $y = x$)

(iterates 100 through 150 for each r)

Figure 6.10 qm > 3.

penetration of a new financial instrument in the niche, from decay to smooth penetration to period doubling cycles and finally to deterministic chaos.

The approach we have taken here opens the way to a wide domain of research from the creation of databases and algorithms to monitor the logistic evolution and the associated change of derivative that marks the passage from the "Malthusian"—exponential growth—phase to the "Verhulstian"—saturation—phase of the logistic curve for each instrument. Moreover, in the space of the decisions to allocate money to financial instruments the trajectories may be represented at any time in relation to the limits of sudden change. Our analysis uses a relatively simple nonlinear approach (probably not so simple from a

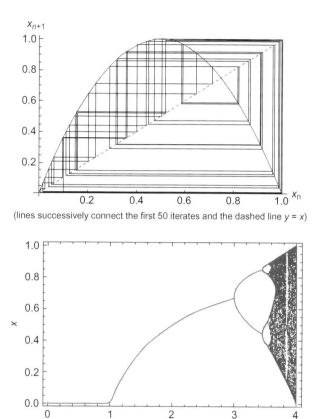

(lines successively connect the first 50 iterates and the dashed line $y = x$)

(iterates 100 through 150 for each r)

Figure 6.11 qm = 4.

linear point of view), but even so, it can describe more types of evolutions including the one generated by discontinuous decisions. More complex many-folds may be generated along with more complex meme behavior, and I hope that once the way has been opened there will be interesting developments ahead.

REFERENCES

Baumol, W.J., Benhabib, J., 1989. Chaos: significance, mechanism, and economic applications. J. Econ. Perspect. 3 (1).

Baumol, W.J., Wolff, E.N., 1983. Feedback from productivity growth to R&D. Scand. J. Econ. 85 (2), 147–157.

Purica, I., 2010. Nonlinear Models for Economic Decision Processes. Imperial College Press, London.

CHAPTER 7

Final Thoughts on Crises and Adaptability

This chapter concludes the book proposing that we need the crises in order to have faster adaptability of the economies to crossing various limits, be they social or environmental ones. The use of the crises as instruments of accelerating adaptation may bring a different approach to development than the present-day exponential one and, also, bring alternative views to growth versus development in a more sustainable world.

Financial activity is based on credibility and, in its turn, this involves the setup of a collective behavior for which great efforts are made to be kept stable. A loss of credibility can destroy a bank or produce drastic drops in the value of shares as well as create discontinuous changes.

Credibility is a dynamic state. It is acquired through the reaction and diffusion of mind entities called memes that penetrate the minds of people in a collectivity and generate a collective behavior that sometimes is very different from the one of the individual. A cultural niche is created associated with each domain of human activity, in this case finance, that contains the memes supporting the financial instruments occupying the niche. New instruments (supported by memes) appear and penetrate the niche to strive for dominating it. The penetration is done to the detriment of other instruments and the process is following a logistic curve.

The logistic curve has two parts in its dynamics. One is an "exponential growth" when the perception is that there are no limits and the other is the "saturation" where the limit capacity of the logistic behavior is reached. The change is similar to a phase change from chemical systems, as it was shown considering the characteristics of meme reactions in the process of creative behavior. Thus, the new financial instrument eventually dominates the market. The domination of the market is actually seen in decisions to allocate more resources to the specific instrument. Monitoring of this dynamic in order to determine the change of phase may be done with the derivative of the logistic function. This has a change from increasing to decreasing as the phase switches to saturation. The change may allow to predict in due time the occurrence of the saturation, hence the discontinuous decision.

The decision is represented as a trajectory that evolves into a folded space where there are control parameters, representing the benefits and the risks associated to the financial instrument. The trajectory is controlled by the values of the parameters and since in the decision space there is a limit of changing behavior given by the folded surface, crossing of that limit by the trajectory, from one fold to the other, is marking the decision to abandon allocating resources to the instrument and divert them to the other instruments in the niche.

This discontinuous decision is perceived as a crisis and there is a changing of the collective behavior that lasts until another new financial instrument penetrates and starts dominating the niche. It seems that there is an asymmetric effect of the "exponential growth" phase in terms of memes, meaning that the collective behavior associated to credibility is restored as if the community had lost memory of the previous crisis cycle. This creates the basis to start a new crisis cycle.

Looking back at the crisis cycle that was described based on the logistic penetration of various memes associated to financial instruments in the banking cultural niche, leading to saturation of the dominant instrument followed by the discontinuous decision to abandon the allocation of resources to that instrument, we end up with the existential question.

7.1 DO WE WANT TO ELIMINATE THE CRISES?

Trying to answer it we are coming again at the dichotomy of local versus global view. Locally speaking, the crisis cycle is bad for most and good for some—voting in a democratic way would result to be bad. If one looks at the global level, another pattern of behavior is taking shape.

First, we live in a world of change. There is a certain "inertia (reluctance) to change" in human structures and that is manifested in dynamic stability far from thermodynamic equilibrium (Purica, 2010).

Second, environment is changing and, in order to adapt, we need, along with resilience, the variability and the capability to change fast (even discontinuously fast sometimes). New discoveries are needed, be they in science, in finance, or in fashion, just to mention extremely different domains of human activity. Variability is needed even if only to provide space for new generations' wishes for affirmation and new things. After the crisis, there is change—sudden and with large amplitude—in various economic sectors and even in economic decision behavior. A first reaction is to control things such as not to have them repeated. Although, there is also, as Galbraith pointed out, an effect of short memory that leads to repeating the main pattern that will generate the next crisis cycle.

This brings to mind a jet fighter that was designed to be inherently unstable and its stability controlled by computers—whenever a fast maneuver was needed the instability was let loose and then stability in the new regime was recontrolled back in.

If this approach is applied to economic systems, the crisis cycle provides a way to have a better adaptability to various changes, for example, climate change. One may remember that after the crisis of large car manufacturers in the USA there was increased production of electrical vehicles; this would not have occurred at the same rate if the economy was on an increase path, because of the inertia toward change that we were talking about earlier.

Analyzing the behavior in the financial niche one should understand that no single financial instrument may give the possibility to predict, but, the behavior of all instruments should be considered. Every once in a while one instrument starts to occupy the niche, and that is the moment when the logistic penetration of that instrument should be monitored in order to determine the change of phase from the "exponential growth" phase to "saturation." Obviously the penetration of one instrument is done to the detriment of another or several others and these have got to be monitored too.

Moreover, there is a decision space where an instrument has a decision trajectory to allocate resources to it during its evolution. This space is having a fold that creates a limit of decision change from allocation of resources to abandoning the specific instrument in favor of others. The decision trajectory in the folded space of the "cusp" may take several paths and the capability to follow them, either toward a local stability point or to the limit of discontinuous change, allows prediction.

The capability to predict gives the possibility to prepare for the change, that is, to avoid it or, if not possible or not wanted, to be resilient to it. Being capable of doing this may introduce a mechanism of self-feedback in the evolution of financial systems. This mechanism is not aimed at avoiding crises but at containing their amplitude and or being able to control their frequency to cope with the system's resilience. The dynamics of the financial niche will always generate dominant instruments and saturation—triggering discontinuous decisions—but having the predictive possibility to control when the limit of change will be approached allows containing the size of the discontinuity.

It is clear that a connection of the flux of money to other fluxes in the economy is needed. The penetration of energy technologies was shown to be also of the same type (a logistic dynamical technological niche). The penetration of information memes is similar and also labor dynamics should be analyzed. One should also look deeper at the evolution of the fluxes of products to see how the natural resources are brought in to manufacturing centers and resulting products are distributed afterward—the cycle being closed by waste treatment. Understanding how these niches mutually influence each other is paramount to generate a science of systems of systems dynamics leading to a better setup for a development, where the dynamics of nature balance the dynamics of human structures.

One may see we have come here to the very definition of sustainable development or, in terms of nonlinear science, to a dynamically complex structure of systems having stable behavior far from equilibrium. The dynamical stability is not about eliminating crisis cycles but integrating them in a global view of the system behavior. As one may see, on a larger time scale, development is not just exponential growth but saturation and change too, and if we seriously want to understand it, we have to consider the big picture too and get accustomed to having limits. Evolution is not about asymptotically reaching the limits but about crossing them into new basins of behavior.

Measuring the effects and monitoring this behavior must lead to complex indicators. If in fluid dynamics we have discovered how to represent the system limits of behavior by complex indicators such as the criterial numbers formed of several correlated physical parameters, it seems that we are not at that level, yet, in finance. Although the equations used to build options and derivatives are typical diffusion equations, there is not an integrated model unifying the process. We should mention here a profound paper by Kreuser and Siegel (1995) showing that derivative securities instruments may be generated as a combination of atomic instruments having various spectral patterns—similar to the buildup of molecules from atoms in chemistry.

One of the conclusions after the 2007 crisis was that there are no models to predict these events. We have tried to look at some models in this book but it seems that the approach to most of them is based on a linear behavior or a quasi-linear one. There are, though, several attempts in the literature to escape the narrow vision normally given by linear models. We say "normally" given because it is typical in the making of a linear model to consider a narrow vicinity around the local point of interest. Obviously, when this point is close to a critical change of phase or a limit of discontinuous behavior, the linear model does not work any longer. One may go to descriptions that synergetically use models from other sciences. An example could be the Bhom's quantum mechanical description that was used to model information dynamics related to given financial systems behavior by Haven (2010), or the description by Purica (2010) of the velocity of rotation of the monetary mass as a typical Schrodinger equation from quantum physics (of course with another meaning of the parameters and variables). There the change is described as the passing of the financial system from one quantum state to another assuming the system may not be in any state but in well-defined ones similar to quantum states in physics. Absorption or emission of money may be similar to absorption or emission of energy in changing the energy levels of a particle.

One basic conclusion is that we are just beginning to describe the behavior in the financial world and since this involves psychology, evolution, reaction-diffusion, phase change, competition in a specific niche, and discontinuous decisions to allocate resources, any attempt to model this behavior should consider all of the above and integrate it in a comprehensive approach. We have tried to do this in a simple (by nonlinear standards) approach with the hope this is somehow the start of a logistic penetration for a different mentality in making "out-of-the-box" integrated approaches to understanding the dynamics of financial and socioeconomic systems' behavior.

Another thing we consider important would be to devise financial behavior that is not based only on an exponential evolution. This would probably involve at least short and long time constants where on short time the behavior is exponential while on long time there may be saturation setting in. In a way, even the time value of money may not be exponential *ad infinitum*. Moreover, a loan for a very long term may generate memes related to the confidence in the capability to have it paid back that are somehow introducing a given kind of saturation. One may think that the future may bring loans that have a given function of debt service that may be logistic or have any other time evolution. The financial instruments will be treated not only independently but also in relation to the behavior of all instruments in the niche, and we may think of instruments connected to climate change and other natural processes—weather derivatives are already in place. Development will be disconnected from energy consumption increase and from greenhouse gases emissions, while the indicators of welfare will not only measure growth but also development, understood in a more complex way, and "crises" will be instruments for a faster adaptation of economies to natural and anthropic changes.

REFERENCES

Haven, E., 2010. The Blackwell and Dubins theorem and Rényi's amount of information measure: some applications. Acta Appl. Math. 109, 743–757. Available from: http://dx.doi.org/10.1007/s10440-008-9343-y.

Kreuser, J., Seigel, L., 1995. Derivative Securities: The Atomic Structure. World Bank Working Papers.

Purica, I., 2010. Nonlinear Models for Economic Decision Processes. Imperial College Press, London.

Evolution of Models in Relation to Crisis Cycles

We live in a real economic world with limits of all sorts and dynamics having various time constants that range from, for example, the tick of the Tokyo stock exchange (8 s) to the maturity of the US Treasury T-bonds (30 years). There are several lines of thinking in the economic literature related to how to describe crises cycles. Depending on where they have originated they are either trying to find some important parameters that directly induce the cyclic behavior or to correlate the dynamics of usually two, or more, variables in obtaining the cyclic behavior, or even to devise process-oriented models based on physical approaches that introduce, for example, different timescale behavior (long and short) that may have cross influences.

One of these thinking lines originates in the Keynesian tradition, for example, Minsky (1975, 1982, 1986), Tobin (1980), Kindleberger and Aliber (2005), and Gallegati et al. (2011). Out of these, especially Minsky was rediscovered after the set of recent crises. But all of them have had a strong influence in analyzing financial crisis cycles. In line with finding specific behavior drivers for this interaction, Shiller (1991, 2001) introduced the overreaction hypothesis. For the most part, the above research is influenced by Keynes' view on the role of "animal spirit" in growth and downturns.

A more recent non-neoclassical tradition, concentrating on negative externalities, originates in work by a Stiglitz-led group of authors. They identify recent developments in information economics, attempting to describe how actual financial markets operate by referring to the concepts of asymmetric information, adverse selection, and moral hazard.

In recent years Steve Keen (2007) works on models that are process description oriented, without trying to identify one or two important parameters, but building a model of the process and looking for various basins of behavior. One of the findings is that there may be dynamic equilibriums associated with those basins that make the notion of thermodynamic equilibrium previously used in economic dynamics become a seldom-occurring situation.

The moment crisis unfolds itself, like the Asian one in the 1990, work starts to be done in order to describe and understand it. Mishkin (1998), for example, has come up with an explanation of the Asian financial crisis of 1997/1998 using an information-theoretic approach. A similar theory, by Krugman (1999a,b), has put the blame on banks' and firms' deteriorating balance sheets. Miller and Stiglitz (1999) employ a multiple-equilibriums model to explain financial crises in general.

These theories point to the perils of too-fast liberalization of financial markets and to the consequent need for government bank supervision and guarantees. From a different angle, Burnside et al. (1999) view government guarantees as real causes of financial crises. They argue that the lack of private hedging of exchange rate risk by firms and banks led to financial crises in Asia.

Another approach, following the bank run model of Diamond and Dybvik (1983), argues that financial crises occur when there is a lack of short-term liquidity. Further description of financial crises generated by exchange rate shocks may be found in Edwards (1999). He goes beyond government and looks at the role of the International Monetary Fund as the lender of last resort. Recent work on the role of currency in financial crises can be found in Kato et al. (2009) and Roethig et al. (2007). These authors follow a macroeconomic approach to describe currency and financial crises and consider the role of currency hedging in mitigating financial crises. See also the papers by Bernanke and Mishkin, Bernanke (1983), Bernanke and Gertler (1994), Bernanke et al. (1998), Mishkin (1998), Bernanke and Blinder (1998), and on the IT bubble, see Semmler (2011, chapter 7).

The idea that government may have a role in the financial crises constitutes a basis for advocating capital markets liberalization. The sustainers of such liberalization mention possible benefits generated by free capital mobility such as: (1) increase of investment returns; (2) reducing trading costs, low costs of financial transaction; (3) increasing liquidity in the financial market; (4) lowering the cost of capital when firms invest; and (5) increasing economic growth and positive employment effects. We have here an example of seeing only the exponential growth phase of the logistic behavior. Liberalized capital markets are only trying to push up the carrying capacity limit such that to delay the moment of changing to the saturation phase. Only this planet is finite and however high, there is still a limit that may be reached. The reaction of liberalization supporters, in the second phase, is (as it had been seen during the housing bubble of 2007) that the governments should come in again and take the "toxic credits" away from the capital market.

In a symmetric way the governments may ask for a total liberalization of the monitoring of the capital markets that would cancel fiscal paradises and would set up taxes on financial transactions wherever these take place. This way the funds to cover the next wave of toxic credits will have been created before this wave strikes with the next crisis. Looking back, we are again in the position of criticizing the governments as risk absorbers that could foster financial crises.

Thus, private risk hedging is probably better, and from a meme point of view the risk-taking behavior would be drastically changed if, for example, the risk coverage would be ensured at the limit (another limit introduced) from the personal assets of all the bank's personnel. When you know you are liable with all your personal assets for the outcome of a given financial instrument innovation on these instruments is usually taking a different path than in the case of no personal risk exposure.

Finally the question arises on private hedging—about how private should the hedging be? To avoid all the situations described above we think prediction may be a good way out. If one can predict risk increase then decisions may be taken to avoid or prepare taking the risk. This way the risk takers, be they private or government, are ready for the future whatever that future is chosen to be.

Going on with models on the housing bubble of 2007, Piazzesi et al. (2007) use a portfolio approach and argue that the fraction of housing assets in households' portfolios went down in the 1980s, whereas the fraction of equity held in those portfolios rose rapidly in the 1990s. Then, the trend reversed, starting in 2000–2001, with a rapid increase in housing assets. They attribute this to the shift in expected returns from three types of assets: fixed income, equity, and real estate. They say that this significant change in asset allocation was related to the inflation rate of the 1980s.

We see here how the variation of various instruments in the niche (associated to the portfolio) is described considering only the time constants of penetration and not the shape of the penetration curve. When considering the parameters in the decision space one is inclined to take only single economic indicators as influencing factors.

We think that the parameters are combined expressions of the single indicators, more like the criterial numbers in the description of fluid flow that are expressions of several physical magnitudes. One may notice here that economy has not reached that level of aggregated parameters, probably due to the fact that the processes are not described using advanced mathematical formulations but just statistics. This level was reached in physics in the times of Tycho Brahe, who was carefully noting the time series (allow me to use present-day's terminology) of the moon positions in the sky. A Newton was needed—and he came latter—to describe the process of the gravitational fields and attraction.

Further on, Shiller (2006, 2007) considers the housing boom to emerge from some overshooting mechanisms and excess volatility, first in the equity market and then, second, in the real estate sector. More specifically, Schiller points out that investors are usually not up to date on the latest economic models. For example, there is a money "illusion" in which investors base their decisions on nominal interest rates when real rates would be more appropriate. Here one is led to think of the model risk included in the VaR methodology, which takes us to the information that one investor may have not only information on the market indicators but also on the models that connect them. This is again an issue of process description and of what may symbolically be called second-order information, that is, information on how to interpret basic information.

The phenomenon is also present in equity markets where price-to-dividend ratios can overshoot their mean values. To analyze this argument in the context of housing markets, one may have to see how this overshooting manifests itself in terms of asset pricing.

In Finicelli (2007) we see that the housing price-to-rent ratio shows a rapid upward deviation from its mean beginning in 2003. More interestingly, we see that by many other measures, for example, the housing price-to-disposable income ratio and debt service-to-personal income ratio have been rising as well since the mid-1990s.

A different line of work goes away from the real estate market, as the basic cause for the current crisis cycle, and attribute the recent events to technology shocks. Several papers use the dynamic stochastic general equilibrium (DSGE) model.

In the context of real business cycles models, technology and technology shocks drive asset prices. So, there have been a few recent studies that try to reconstruct crisis cycles using RBC models with misperceived technology shocks as driving force. Here, a time delay in the actual implementation of technology, after the perception of a technology shock, is seen as the factor for the crisis cycle; see Beaudry and Portier (2004), Christiano et al. (2006, 2007), and Lansing (2008). In most of these papers, the expectation dynamics concern the technology shocks, which, however, are likely to explain only part of the crisis cycle in asset markets.

A high-impact model, along the line of a DSGE approach, has been proposed by Bernanke et al. (1998). This is the financial accelerator model that proposes that credit cost and credit volume move procyclically, having an amplifying effect on the ups and downs of real activities. Basically, this is collateralized borrowing: with asset prices high, net worth will be high, and collateralized borrowing is stimulated. The reverse is supposed to happen in downturns.

This approach proposes that spread of credit cost and credit volume depends upon asset prices that can indeed show local spike effects on the ups and downs of real activities. Yet, there is some incertitude on the collateral, the borrowing constraints, since they are supposed to be represented by the discounted expected pay-offs. The constraints become, in fact, some speculative constraint. Moreover, the evolution of leveraging is usually not monitored and the impact of leveraging, on asset prices, is seldom studied. The interaction of asset prices and leveraging is not fully modeled in the financial accelerator approach.

Various other sources of information may be mentioned such as the extensive survey of Goodhart and Hofmann (2003); the historical studies on financial crises by Minsky (1975, 1982, 1986) and Kindleberger and Aliber (2005), and also recent dynamic models such as Brunnermeier and Sannikov (2010), Geanakoplos (2010), Miller and Stiglitz (2010), Keen (2007), and Hall (2010, 2011).

One other interesting approach is done by Haven (2010), where three key features of Bohmian mechanics are used, that is, (i) Bohmian mechanics allows the wave function to be interpreted as an information function; (ii) Bohmian mechanics provides for the possibility of having trajectories; and (iii) Bohmian mechanics provides for nonlocality. In this context an interesting interpretation is developed, from an economics point of view: if one replaces the wave function by an information wave function and the particle by an asset price, then, a formalism, originating from physics, is obtained, which can be used beneficially (in quantum-like terms) in an economics (asset pricing) context.

REFERENCES

Beaudry, P., Portier, F., 2004. When Can Changes in Expectations Cause Business Cycle Fluctuations in Neo-Classical Settings? Center for Economic and Policy Research Discussion Paper No. 4628.

Bernanke, B., 1983. Nonmonetary effects of the financial crisis in the propagation of the great depression. Am. Econ. Rev. 73 (June), 257–276.

Bernanke, B., Blinder, A., 1998. Credit, money, and aggregate demand. Am. Econ. Rev. 78, 435–439.

Bernanke, B., Gertler, M., 1994. The financial accelerator and the flight to quality. Rev. Econ. Stat. 78 (1), 1–15.

Bernanke, B., Gertler, M., Gilchrist, S., 1998. The financial accelerator in a quantitative business cycle framework. National Bureau of Economic Research Working Paper No. 6455. In: Taylor, J., Woodford, M. (Eds.), Handbook of Macroeconomics. North-Holland, Amsterdam.

Brunnermeier, M., Sannikov, Y., 2010. A Macroeconomic Model with a Financial Sector. Working Paper, Princeton University.

Burnside, C., Eichenbaum, M., Rebelo, S., 1999. Hedging and financial fragility in fixed exchange rate regimes. Eur. Econ. Rev. 45, 1151–1193.

Christiano, L., Motto, R., Rostagno, M., 2006. Monetary Policy and Stock Market Boom–Bust Cycles. Working Paper.

Christiano, L., Motto, R., Rostagno, M., 2007. Two Reasons Why Money and Credit May Be Useful in Monetary Policy. Working Paper.

Diamond, P., Dybvik, P., 1983. Bank runs, deposit insurance and liquidity. J. Polit. Econ. 91 (June), 401–419.

Edwards, S., 1999. On Crisis Prevention: Lessons From Mexico and East Asia. National Bureau of Economic Research Working Paper No. 7233.

Finicelli, A., 2007. House Price Developments and Fundamentals in the United States. Bank of Italy Occasional Paper No. 7.

Hall, R., 2010. Forward-Looking Decision Making. Princeton University Press, Princeton, NJ.

Hall, R., 2011. The long slump. Am. Econ. Rev 101 (2), 431–469. Available from: http://dx.doi .org/10.1257/aer.101.2.431.

Haven, E., 2010. The Blackwell and Dubins theorem and Rényi's amount of information measure: some applications. Acta Appl. Math. 109, 743–757. Available from: http://dx.doi.org/10.1007/s10440-008-9343-y.

Gallegati, M., Palestrini, A., Rosser Jr., J.B., 2011. The period of financial distress in speculative markets: interacting heterogeneous agents and financial constraints. Macroecon. Dyn. 15, 60–79.

Geanakoplos, J., 2010. Solving the Present Crisis and Managing the Leverage Cycle. Federal Reserve Bank of New York Economic Policy Review, August, pp. 101–131.

Goodhart, C., Hofmann, B., 2003. Deflation, Credit and Asset Prices. Working Paper.

Kato, M., Proano, C., Semmler, W., 2009. Capital Flight, Nominal Exchange Rate Volatility and Optimal International Reserves Management. Working Paper.

Keen, S., 2007. Debunking Economics. Zed Books, New York, ISBN: 978-1-85649-991-0.

Kindleberger, C., Aliber, R., 2005. Manias, Panics, and Crashes: A History of Financial Crises, fifth ed. Wiley, New York, NY.

Krugman, P., 1999a. Balance sheets, the transfer problem and financial crises. J. Money Credit Banking 11, 311–325.

Krugman, P., 1999b. Comments on the Transfer Problem. MIT, mimeo.

Lansing, K., 2008. Speculative Growth and Overreaction to Technology Shocks. Federal Reserve Bank of San Francisco Working Paper 2008-08.

Miller, M., Stiglitz, J., 1999. Bankruptcy Protection Against Macroeconomic Shocks. The World Bank, mimeo.

Miller, M., Stiglitz, J., 2010. Leverage and asset bubbles: averting armageddon with chapter 11? Econ. J. 120 (544), 500–518.

Minsky, H., 1975. John Maynard Keynes. Columbia University Press, New York, NY.

Minsky, H., 1982. Can It Happen Again? ME Sharpe, Armonk, NY.

Minsky, H., 1986. Stabilizing an Unstable Economy. Yale University Press, New Haven, CT.

Mishkin, F., 1998. International Capital Movement, Financial Volatility and Financial Instability. National Bureau of Economic Research Working Paper.

Piazzesi, M., Schneider, M., Tuzel, S., 2007. Housing, consumption and asset pricing. J. Fin. Econ. 83 (3), 531–569.

Roethig, A., Semmler, W., Flaschel, P., 2007. Hedging, speculation, and investment in balance-sheet triggered currency crises. Australian Econ Papers 46 (3), 224–233.

Semmler, W., 2011. Asset Prices, Booms and Recessions: Financial Economics from a Dynamic Perspective, third ed. Springer Publishing House, New York, NY.

Shiller, R., 1991. Market Volatility. MIT Press, Cambridge, MA.

Shiller, R., 2001. Irrational Exuberance. Random House, New York, NY.

Shiller, R., 2006. Long-term perspectives on the current boom in home prices. Economists' Voice 3 (4).

Shiller, R., 2007. Low Interest Rates and High Asset Prices: An Interpretation in Terms of Changing Popular Models. Working Paper.

Tobin, J., 1980. Asset Accumulation and Economic Activity. Basic Blackwell, Oxford.

APPENDIX 2

Logistic Map

The literature abounds in various presentations of this topic and we have chosen one that allows the reader to get accustomed with the specific behavior and also gives a wide range of references for those who want to study more.

We have selected here some basic elements of the logistic map. For a more detailed explanation we recommend: Weisstein, E.W. "Logistic Map." From *MathWorld*—A Wolfram Web Resource. http://mathworld. wolfram.com/LogisticMap.html.

The so-called logistic map results from replacing the logistic equation:

$$\frac{\mathrm{d}x}{\mathrm{d}t} = rx(1 - x) \qquad (A2.1)$$

with the quadratic recurrence equation:

$$x_{n+1} = rx_n(1 - x_n) \qquad (A2.2)$$

where r is a positive constant.

This quadratic map may describe very complicated behavior. The work by W. Ricker in 1954 and detailed analytic studies of logistic maps beginning in the 1950s with Paul Stein and Stanislaw Ulam underlined the properties of this type of map beyond simple oscillatory behavior (Wolfram, 2002, pp. 918–919).

The graphical representation of the quadratic recurrence equation is given below. Two values for r are selected ($y = rx(1 - x)$), one in the bifurcation area and the other one in the chaotic behavior area. There are such diagrams that can be done for every value in the interval. The important thing to consider is the fact that there are several types of behavior ranging from convergence to zero to smooth, to oscillatory and, finally, to chaotic behavior (Figure A2.1).

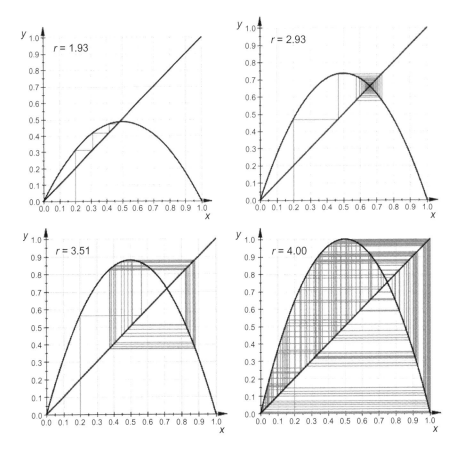

Figure A2.1 Selected behavior of the logistic map.

Figure A2.2 shows a bifurcation diagram of the logistic map resulting from plotting, as a function of r, a series of values for x_n obtained by starting with a random value x_0, iterating many times, and discarding the first points corresponding to values before the iterates converge to the attractor. In other words, the set of fixed points of x_n corresponding to a given value of r is plotted for values of r increasing to the right.

In order to study the fixed points of the logistic map, let an initial point, x_0, lie in the interval [0, 1]. Then find appropriate conditions on r that keep points in the interval. The maximum value x_{n+1} can take is found from

$$\frac{dx_{n+1}}{dx_n} = r(1 - 2x_n) = 0 \qquad (A2.3)$$

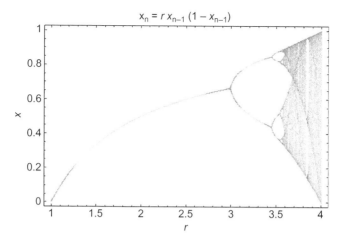

Figure A2.2 Logistic map   through bifurcation to chaos.

so the largest value of x_{n+1} occurs for $x_n = 1/2$. Plugging this in, $\max(x_{n+1}) = r/4$. Therefore, to keep the map in the desired region, we must have $r \in [0, 4]$. The Jacobian is:

$$J = \left| \frac{\mathrm{d}x_{n+1}}{\mathrm{d}x_n} \right| = |r(1 - 2x_n)| \qquad (A2.4)$$

and the map is stable at a point x_0 if $J(x_0) < 1$.

As the r value increases n-cycles are occurring.

The following table summarizes the values r_n at which the n-cycle first appears. For $n = 1, 2,\ldots$, these have algebraic degrees 1, 1, 2, 2, 22, 40, 114, 12,... (Sloane's A118454).

N	Deg (r_n)	Sloane	Value
1	1		1
2	1		3
3	2	A086178	3.82842712...
4	2	A086180	3.44948974...
5	22	A118452	3.73817237...
6	40	A118453	3.62655316...
7	114	A118746	3.70164076...
8	12	A086181	3.54409035...
9			
10			
16	240	A091517	3.56440726...

The algebraic orders of the values of r_2^n (i.e., the onset of the 2^n-cycle) for $n = 1, 2, \ldots$ are therefore given by 1, 2, 12, 240,... (Sloane's A087046). A table of the cycle type and value of r_2^n at which the cycle 2^n appears is given below.

n	Cycle (2^n)	r_2^n	Sloane
1	2	3	
2	4	3.449490	A086180
3	8	3.544090	A086181
4	16	3.564407	A091517
5	32	3.568750	
6	64	3.56969	
7	128	3.56989	
8	256	3.569934	
9	512	3.569943	
10	1024	3.5699451	
11	2048	3.569945557	
∞	Accumulation point	3.569945672	A098587

For additional values, see Rasband (1990, p. 23). The period doubling bifurcations come faster and faster (8, 16, 32,...), then suddenly break off. Beyond a certain point known as the accumulation point, periodicity gives way to chaos, as illustrated below. In the middle of the complexity, a window suddenly appears with a regular period like 3 or 7 as a result of mode locking. The period-3 bifurcation occurs at $r = 1 + 2\sqrt{2} = 3.828427\ldots$, and period doublings then begin again with cycles of 6, 12,... and 7, 14, 28,..., and then once again break off to chaos. However, note that considerable structure can be found within this chaos (Mayoral and Robledo, 2005a,b).

It is shown that the logistic map is chaotic on an invariant Cantor set for $r > 2 + \sqrt{5} \approx 4.236$ (Devaney, 1989, pp. 31–50; Gulick, 1992, pp. 112–126; Holmgren, 1996, pp. 69–85), but in fact, it is also chaotic for all $r > 4$ (Kraft, 1999; Robinson, 1995, pp. 33–37).

The logistic map has correlation exponent 0.500 ± 0.005 (Grassberger and Procaccia, 1983), capacity dimension 0.538 (Grassberger, 1981), and information dimension 0.5170976 (Grassberger and Procaccia, 1983).

REFERENCES

Devaney, R., 1989. An Introduction to Chaotic Dynamical Systems, second ed. Addison-Wesley, Redwood City, CA.

Grassberger, P., 1981. On the Hausdorff dimension of fractal attractors. J. Stat. Phys. 26, 173–179.

Grassberger, P., Procaccia, I., 1983. Measuring the strangeness of strange attractors. Physica D 9, 189–208.

Gulick, D., 1992. Encounters with Chaos. McGraw-Hill, New York, NY.

Holmgren, R., 1996. A First Course in Discrete Dynamical Systems, second ed. Springer-Verlag, New York, NY.

Kraft, R.L., 1999. Chaos, cantor sets, and hyperbolicity for the logistic maps. Amer. Math. Monthly 106, 400–408.

Mayoral, E., Robledo, A., January 17, 2005a. A recent appreciation of the singular dynamics at the edge of chaos. <http://arxiv.org/abs/cond-mat/0501398>.

Mayoral, E., Robledo, A., 2005b. Tsallis' q index and Mori's q phase transitions at edge of chaos. Phys. Rev. E 72, 026209.

Rasband, S.N., 1990. Chaotic Dynamics of Nonlinear Systems. Wiley, New York, NY.

Robinson, C., 1995. Stability, Symbolic Dynamics, and Chaos. CRC Press, Boca Raton, FL.

Sloane, N.J.A., Sequences A086178, A086179, A086180, A086181, A087046, A091517, A098587, A118452, A118453, A118454, and A118746 in The On-Line Encyclopedia of Integer Sequences.

Wolfram, S., 2002. A New Kind of Science. Wolfram Media, Champaign, IL, pp. 918–921 and 1098.

Wolfram Research, Inc., Logistic Map. <http://documents.wolfram.com/mathematica/Demos/SoundGallery/LogisticMap.html>.

BIBLIOGRAPHY

Adams, K., Marcet, A., 2010. Booms and Busts in Asset Prices. Institute for Monetary and Economic Studies Discussion Paper Series. <http://www.imes.boj.or.jp/research/papers/english/10-E-02.pdf>.

Adrian, T., Shin, H., 2009. Money, liquidity, and monetary policy. Am. Econ. Rev. 99 (May 2), 600–605.

Akkeren, M., Hansen, H., 2004. On mortgage prepayment and default: a historical distribution analysis approach. In: AFIR Colloquium, Boston, MA, USA, November 8–10.

Allen, R.E., 1989. Globalization of the US financial markets: the new structure for monetary policy. International Economics and Financial Markets: The AMEX Bank Review Prize Essays. Oxford University Press, Oxford.

Allen, R.E. (Ed.), 2004. The Political Economy of Financial Crisis. Edward Elgar, Northampton, MA.

Bailey, D.H., 1993. Multiprecision translation and execution of fortran programs. ACM Trans. Math. Software 19, 288–319.

Bailey, D.H., Broadhurst, D.J., 2000. Parallel integer relation detection: techniques and applications. Math. Comput. 70, 1719–1736.

Bailey, D.H., Borwein, J.M., Kapoor, V., Weisstein, E.W., 2006. Ten problems in experimental mathematics. Amer. Math. Monthly 113, 481–509.

Bailey, D.H., Borwein, J.M., Calkin, N.J., Girgensohn, R., Luke, D.R., Moll, V.H., 2007. Bifurcation points in chaos theory. §2.3.2 in Experimental Mathematics in Action. A K Peters, Wellesley, MA.

Bechhoeffer, J., 1996. The birth of period 3, revisited. Math. Mag 69, 115–118.

Beck, C., Schlögl, F., 1993. Thermodynamics of Chaotic Systems. Cambridge University Press, Cambridge.

Beja, A., Goldman, M., 1980. On the dynamic behaviour of prices in disequilibrium. J. Finance 34, 235–247.

Blundell-Wignall, A., Atkinson, P., 2008. The sub-prime crisis: causal distortions and regulatory reform. In: Bloxham, P., Kent, C. (Eds.), Lessons from the Financial Turmoil of 2007 and 2008. Reserve Bank of Australia.

Bogomolny, A. Chaos Creation (There is Order in Chaos). <http://www.cut-the-knot.org/blue/chaos.shtml>.

Borwein, J., Bailey, D., 2003. Bifurcation points in the logistic iteration. §2.3 in Mathematics by Experiment: Plausible Reasoning in the 21st Century. A K Peters, Wellesley, MA, pp. 50–53.

Brunnermeier, M., 2009. Deciphering the liquidity and credit crunch 2007–2008. J. Econ. Perspect. 23 (Winter 1), 77–100.

Cappuzzo-Dolcetta, I., 1983. On a discrete approximation of the Hamilton–Jacobi equation of dynamic programming. Appl. Math. Optim. 10, 367–377.

Cerny, P.G., 1993. The political economy of international finance. In: Cerny, P.G. (Ed.), Finance and World Politics. Edward Elgar, Brookfield, VT, pp. 3–19.

Chacko, G., Sjoman, A., Motohashi, H., Dessain, V., 2006. Credit Derivatives: A Primer on Credit Risk, Modeling, and Instruments. Wharton School Publishing, Upper Saddle River, NJ.

Chiarella, C., Flaschel, P., Franke, R., Semmler, W., 2009. Financial Markets and the Macroeconomy: A Keynesian Perspective. Routledge International Studies in Money and Banking, Routledge Publishing, New York, NY.

Clarke, S., 1994. Marx's Theory of Crisis. St Martin's Press, New York, NY.

Cochrane, J., 2001. Asset Pricing. Princeton University Press, Princeton, NJ.

Costa, U.M.S., Lyra, M.L., Plastino, A.R., Tsallis, C., 1997. Power-law sensitivity to initial conditions within a logistic-like family of maps: fractality and nonextensivity. Phys. Rev. E 56, 245−250.

Curdia, V., Woodford, M., 2009. Credit Spreads and Monetary Policy. National Bureau of Economic Research, Working Paper No. 15289.

Darwin, C., 1859. On the Origin of Species by Means of Natural Selection. Murray, London (and Penguin, 1968).

Dawkins, R., 1996. Viruses. In: Stocker, G., Schöpf, C. (Eds.), Memesis: The Future of Evolution. Ars Electronica.

Dickau, R.M. Bifurcation Diagram. <http://mathforum.org/advanced/robertd/bifurcation.html>.

Elaydi, S.N., 2000. Discrete Chaos. Chapman & Hall, Boca Raton, FL.

Falcone, M., 1987. A numerical approach to the infinite horizon problem of deterministic control theory. Appl. Math. Optim. 15 (1−13), 213−214.

Federal Reserve Bank of St Louis, 1998. International Economic Trends, August.

Fisher, I., 1933. The debt-deflation theory of great depressions. Econometrica I, 337−357.

Geanakoplos, J., 2009. The leverage cycle. In: Acemoglu, D., Rogoff, K., Woodford, M. (Eds.), National Bureau of Economic Research Macroeconomics Annual, vol. 24. University of Chicago Press, Chicago, IL, pp. 1−65.

Gilchrist, S., Yankov, V., Zakrajsek, E., 2009. Credit Market Shocks and Economic Fluctuations. J. Monet. Econ. 56 (4), 471−493.

Gleick, J., 1988. Chaos: Making a New Science. Penguin Books, New York, NY, pp. 69−80.

Gordon, W.B., 1996. Period three trajectories of the logistic map. Math. Mag. 69, 118−120.

Gorton, G., 2009. Information, Liquidity, and the (Ongoing) Panic of 2007. Prepared for the Federal Reserve Bank of Kansas City, Jackson Hole Conference, August.

Grundfest, J.A., 1991. When markets crash: the consequences of information failure in the market for liquidity. In: Feldstein, M. (Ed.), The Risk of Economic Crisis. The University of Chicago Press, Chicago, IL.

Gruene, L., 1997. An adaptive grid scheme for the discrete Hamilton−Jacobi−Bellman equation. Numerische Mathematik 75, 319−337.

Greenspan, A., 1998. The globalization of finance. Cato J. 17 (3), 243−256.

Gruene, L., Semmler, W., 2004. Using dynamic programming with adaptive grid scheme for optimal control problems in economics. J. Econ. Dyn. Control 28, 2427−2456.

Gruene, L., Semmler, W., 2008. Asset pricing with loss aversion. J. Econ. Dyn. Control 32 (10), 3253−3274.

Gruene, L., Semmler, W., Sieveking, M., 2005. Creditworthiness and threshold in a credit market model with multiple equilibria. Econ. Theory 25 (2), 287−315.

Gruene, L., Semmler, W., Bernard, L., 2007. Firm value, diversified capital assets and credit risk. J. Credit Risk 3 (Winter 4), 81−113.

Gruene, L., Chen. P., Semmler, W., 2008. Boom Bust Cycles, Default Premia and Asset Pricing, Working Paper. <http://www.newschool.edu/nssr/cem>.

Gruene, L., Ohrlein, C., Semmler, W., 2009. Dynamic consumption and portfolio decisions with time varying asset returns. J. Wealth Manage. 12 (2), 21–47.

Haken, H., 2004. Synergetics, Introduction and Advanced Topics. Springer Verlag, Berlin, ISBN 354040824X.

Hall, R., 2010. Forward Looking Decision Making. Princeton Universtiy Press, Princeton, NJ.

Helleiner, E., 1995. Explaining the globalization of financial markets: bringing states back in. Rev. Int. Polit. Econ. 2 (2), 315–341.

Hsiao, C., Semmler, W., 2009. Harmonic Fitting for Long Run Economic Data, Working Paper. <http://www.newschool.edu/nssr/cem/>.

Huang, K., 1963. Statistical Mechanics. Wiley, New York, NY.

Hudson, N., 2006. The new road to serfdom. Harper's Magazine, May.

Jaffe, S. The Logistic Equation: Computable Chaos. <http://library.wolfram.com/infocenter/MathSource/579/>.

Kalecki, M., 1937. The principle of increasing risk. Economica, November, pp. 441–447.

Kaufman, H., 2009. The Road to Financial Reformation: Warnings, Consequences, Reforms. Wiley, New York, NY.

Keynes, J.M., 1936. The General Theory of Employment, Interest, and Money. Macmillan, London.

Kindleberger, C., Aliber, R., 2005. Manias, Panics, and Crashes: A History of Financial Crises, fifth ed. Wiley, New York, NY.

Kotsireas, I.S., Karamanos, K., 2004. Exact computation of the bifurcation point b_4 of the logistic map and the Bailey–Broadhurst conjectures. Int. J. Bifurcation Chaos 14, 2417–2423, <http://www.lacim.uqam.ca/~plouffe/OEIS/archive_in_pdf/costas-cecm.pdf>.

Krugman, P., 1999. Balance Sheets, the Transfer Problem and Financial Crises. MIT, mimeo.

Latora, V., Rapisarda, A., Tsallis, C., Baranger, M., 2000. The rate of entropy increase at the edge of chaos. Phys. Lett. A 273, 97.

Lauwerier, H., 1991. Fractals: Endlessly Repeated Geometrical Figures. Princeton University Press, Princeton, NJ.

Mankiw, G., Weil, D., 1989. The baby boom, the baby bust and the housing market. Reg. Sci. Urban Econ. 19, 235–258.

Marchionatti, R., 1999. On Keynes' animal spirits. Kyklos 52 (3), 415–439.

MathPages. Closed Forms for the Logistic Map. <http://www.mathpages.com/home/kmath188.htm>.

Maurer, H., Semmler, W., 2010. An optimal control model of oil discovery and extraction. Appl. Math. Comput. 217 (3), 1163–1169.

May, R.M., 1976. Simple mathematical models with very complicated dynamics. Nature 261, 459–467.

Merton, R., 1974. On the pricing of corporate debt: the risk structure of the interest rate. J. Finance 2, 449–470.

Mittnik, S., Semmler, W., 2010. Regime Dependence of the Fiscal Multiplier. Schwartz Center for Economic Policy Analysis, Working Paper.

Nicolis, G., Prigogine, I., 1977. Self-Organization in Nonequilibrium Systems. Wiley, London.

Nitzan, J., 1998. Differential accumulation: towards a new political economy of capital. Rev. Int. Polit. Econ. 5 (2), Summer.

Packel, E., 1996. Mathematica for Mathematics Teachers. Institute of Computation.

Pearl, R., 1978. The Biology of Population Growth. Knopf, New York, NY, Chapter 18.

Peitgen, H.-O., Jürgens, H., Saupe, D., 1992. Chaos and Fractals: New Frontiers of Science. Springer-Verlag, New York, NY.

Piazzesi, M., Schneider, M., 2008a. Inflation and the Price of Real Assets, Working Paper.

Piazzesi, M., Schneider, M., 2008b. Inflation illusion, credit, and asset pricing. In: Campbell, J. (Ed.), Asset Prices and Monetary Policy. University of Chicago Press, Chicago, IL.

Quetelet, A., Verhulst, P.F., 1850. Annuaire de l'Académie royale des sciences de Belgique 16, 97–124.

Ramasubramanian, K., Sriram, M.S., September 17, 1999. A Comparative Study of Computation of Lyapunov Spectra with Different Algorithms. <http://arxiv.org/abs/chao-dyn/9909029>.

Review of International Political Economy, 1994. Vol. 1, No. 1, Spring.

Review of International Political Economy, 1996. Vol. 3, No. 3, pp. 528–537.

Rifkin, J., Howard, T., 1980. Entropy: A New World View. The Viking Press, New York, NY, p. 33.

Russell, D.A., Hanson, J.D., Ott, E., 1980. Dimension of strange attractors. Phys. Rev. Let. 45, 1175–1178.

Saha, P., Strogatz, S.H., 1995. The birth of period three. Math. Mag. 68, 42–47.

Semmler, W., Bernard, L. (Eds.), 2007. The Foundations of Credit Risk Analysis. Edward Elgar Publishing, Cheltenham, UK.

Semmler, W., Sieveking, M., 2000. Critical debt and debt dynamics. J. Econ. Dyn. Control 24 (5–7), 1–24.

Soddy, F., 1926. Wealth, Virtual Wealth and Debt. George Allen & Unwin, New York, NY.

Strogatz, S.H., 1994. Nonlinear Dynamics and Chaos. Addison-Wesley, Reading, MA.

Tabor, M., 1989. Chaos and Integrability in Nonlinear Dynamics: An Introduction. Wiley, New York, NY.

Trott, M., 2004. The Mathematica GuideBook for Programming. Springer-Verlag, New York, NY, pp. 24–25, <http://www.mathematicaguidebooks.org/>.

Tsallis, C., Plastino, A.R., Zheng, W.-M., 1997. Power-law sensitivity to initial conditions—new entropic representation. Chaos, Solitons Fractals 8, 885–891.

Ursu I., Vamanu D., 1979. Motivations and Attitudes in the Long-Term Planning of Alternative Energy Systems. Proceeding of the UNITAR Conference on Long-Term Energy Resources, 11, CF7/XXI/2.

Veblen, T., 1923. Absentee Ownership and Business Enterprise in Recent Times. The Case of America, Introduction by Robert Leckachman. Beacon Press, Boston, MA (reproduced 1967).

Wagon, S., 1991. The dynamics of the quadratic map. §4.4 in Mathematica in Action. W. H. Freeman, New York, NY.

Weisstein, E.W. Logistic Map. From MathWorld—A Wolfram Web Resource. <http://mathworld.wolfram.com/LogisticMap.html>.

Made in the USA
Middletown, DE
25 January 2022

59580749R00071